BREAK POINT

orca sports

BREAK POINT

KATE JAIMET

ORCA BOOK PUBLISHERS

Library and Archives Canada Cataloguing in Publication

Jaimet, Kate, 1969-
Break point / Kate Jaimet.
(Orca sports)

Issued also in electronic formats.
ISBN 978-1-4598-0352-7

I. Title. II. Series: Orca sports
PS8619.A368B74 2013   jC813'.6   C2012-907477-2

First published in the United States, 2013
Library of Congress Control Number: 2012952955

Summary: When Connor and Maddy discover that their tennis club is
going bankrupt, they set out to try and save it.

*Orca Book Publishers is dedicated to preserving the environment and has printed
this book on Forest Stewardship Council® certified paper.*

Orca Book Publishers gratefully acknowledges the support for its publishing
programs provided by the following agencies: the Government of Canada through
the Canada Book Fund and the Canada Council for the Arts, and the Province of
British Columbia through the BC Arts Council and
the Book Publishing Tax Credit.

Cover photography by Getty Images
Author photo by John Major

ORCA BOOK PUBLISHERS
PO Box 5626, Stn. B
Victoria, BC Canada
V8R 6S4

ORCA BOOK PUBLISHERS
PO Box 468
Custer, WA USA
98240-0468

www.orcabook.com
Printed and bound in Canada.

16 15 14 13 • 4 3 2 1

For my husband, Mark

chapter one

Maddy raised her hand to her mouth.

"What are we going to do, Connor?" she said. "What are we going to tell my mom?"

I looked at the wreckage in the common room. It was hard to believe this was the same place Maddy and I had spent hours organizing the night before. Vintage tennis rackets lay smashed amid a jumble of overturned chairs. Mangled mannequins were knocked to the floor, their antique tennis clothing slashed to rags. Strewn over everything were shredded bits of paper that had once been autographed photos of famous players.

"Looks like someone broke in," I said.

"Who would do a thing like this?" Said Maddy.

I picked my way toward the back of the room, where a row of windows looked out on the second-floor balcony of the club-house. Shards of broken glass jutted from the wooden window frames. Shattered glass lay on the floor beneath. I peered through one of the smashed windows, as though I expected to see the vandals running away across the back courts. But whoever they were, they were long gone. They must have struck in the middle of the night.

The rising sun turned the sky Easter-egg pink. Mist hung over the tennis courts, and over the river that formed the back border of the Bytowne Tennis Club property. Birds called to each other in reedy voices. It was going to be a beautiful day.

I was going to get the guys who had done this.

I turned back to face the common room. Maddy was crouched amid the pile of broken stuff, holding a smashed tennis racket. It was a Slazenger Challenge #1, a vintage racket from the 1970s. The strings hung loose from its splintered frame. Worst of all, the grip was snapped in two, destroying the autograph scrawled on the wood: Björn Borg.

Borg was one of the greatest tennis players of all time, winner of five Wimbledon trophies and seven Davis Cups. He had played with that racket in the 1974 Italian Championships, when he'd won the singles title at age seventeen, the youngest player ever to take the prize.

"We could've got at least a thousand dollars for this, Connor," Maddy said.

"I'm calling the cops," I answered.

I was heading for the phone when the sound of a car on the street below made me freeze. The car puttered along in low gear, then growled to a stop. The engine shut off with a sigh.

"It's my mom," said Maddy. She turned her brown eyes toward me with a desperate look.

"I'll go down and meet her," I said.

"Would you?" she asked. "I'll call the police."

I nodded and headed toward the staircase. I was acting on an impulse to help Maddy. But truthfully, I didn't know what to say to her mom either. I ran down the stairs two at a time and opened the front door of the clubhouse.

The street was quiet, the houses dark with sleep. A crow flew, cawing, from a rooftop and landed in one of the big, leafy trees that lined the sidewalk. Aside from that, the only movement in the street was the door of Mrs. Sharma's Volkswagen Jetta swinging open.

"Good morning, Connor!" Mrs. Sharma called cheerily as she climbed out from behind the wheel. She waved with one hand, took a large purse out of the car with the other and shut the door with a flick of her hip. She was all glammed up in high heels, a red silk dress and gold jewelry. Her hair, long and black like Maddy's, was pinned up in a complicated style of tucks and swirls. The faint foreign lilt to her voice and the gold bangles that jingled on her bronzed arms made her seem exotic and intimidating. I waved back, feeling too dumb to speak.

It was the first time I had seen her dressed up like that. Even though she was the general manager of the club, Mrs. Sharma usually came to work in khakis and a polo shirt. Her ritzy outfit was clearly meant to impress the wealthy bidders who would be arriving at noon for the vintage tennis auction.

Except now those wealthy bidders wouldn't be arriving. Now, we would have to call the whole thing off.

"Good morning, Mrs. Sharma," I said as she came toward me.

"Connor." She took my hand and squeezed it. "It's so sweet of you to come early and help Madhavi and me get ready."

She breezed past me into the clubhouse.

"Mrs. Sharma, there's a problem." I choked the words out, speaking to the back of her fancy hairdo.

"Don't tell me the auction house wants to send that man Bismuth!" she called over her shoulder. "I told them, I want Walker! I was on the phone for an hour last night, sorting this out!"

By now Mrs. Sharma was halfway up the staircase. I ran to overtake her, but the old wooden steps were so narrow I couldn't pass without shoving her aside. I came up behind her instead. As she reached the top and stepped through the door into the common room, Mrs. Sharma stopped in her tracks.

"Oh God," she said.

She raised her hand to her mouth. It was the same gesture Maddy had made. She staggered sideways. She was about to stumble into an overturned chair when Maddy caught her by the arm. I grabbed a chair from the heap and set it upright for her to sit on.

"It's ruined," Mrs. Sharma said. The look in her eyes was like something inside her had just been shattered—shattered as badly as the Slazenger tennis racket. "Everything is ruined."

chapter two

Ten minutes later the police arrived, followed by an appraisal guy from the insurance company. The two officers had a quick look around the scene. Then Maddy and I took them down to the front desk and showed them the security videotape from the night before. Meanwhile, Maddy's mom went through a list of the vandalized items with the insurance agent. We had already posted notices on the front door and on the club's website that the auction had been cancelled due to "unforeseen circumstances."

The grainy black-and-white footage of the security video showed five people, all wearing ski masks and gloves, walking across the small parking area in front of the club. They looked like teenage guys, from the clothes they were wearing—baggy pants slung low around their hips, hoodies and sneakers with the laces undone. The guys stopped at the chain-link fence that encircled the grounds and had some kind of a discussion. Then they climbed the fence and moved out of range of the camera. It was easy to imagine them climbing the back staircase of the club-house to the balcony and smashing the windows to get inside.

"Doesn't look like we'll get any ID from that tape," one of the policemen said as Maddy's mom came up behind us. "We'll go through the scene to see if they left anything behind. Footprints. Fingerprints. Personal items. You never know." The officer turned to Mrs. Sharma.

"Do you have an estimate of the value of the items that were damaged?" he asked.

"I was thinking around a hundred thousand," she said. "The insurance company estimate is...substantially lower."

"Isn't it always," the police officer commented.

"I wouldn't know," said Mrs. Sharma. "I've never dealt with a situation like this before."

"I'm sorry, ma'am," he said. "Who did the items belong to?"

"They were donated by club members for a fundraising auction. Some of them were one of a kind, you know. There was a program from the 1931 Wimbledon. And several autographed tennis rackets. I've already had donors calling me, wanting to know why the auction's been cancelled. They're quite upset. They want compensation, some of them. They're saying they didn't donate their valuable property to see it destroyed. They think the club should have taken better care..."

Maddy took her mother's hand.

"I'm sorry we can't help you with compensation, ma'am," said the officer. "If the items had been stolen, we might have been able to recover the goods. You'd be surprised what people will try to sell on eBay. But in this situation—"

"I don't understand," Mrs. Sharma said. "Why would anyone do this?"

"Do you know anyone who would want to target the club?" one of the policemen asked.

"Target the club? No. I have no idea."

"It might be a random act of vandalism, then. These things happen. Sad to say, but some people have no respect for other people's property."

After a few more questions, Mrs. Sharma led the officers up to the common room to go through the crime scene. Maddy and I sat at the club's front desk for a while, not saying anything. I couldn't think of anything more we could do.

"Want to hit some balls?" I asked.

"I don't know. It doesn't feel right." Maddy shrugged. "Let's go for a walk instead."

I understood her point. If people saw us playing tennis, they would think we didn't care about the stuff that had gotten ruined. They would think we were just out there having fun. But that wasn't how I saw it.

Whenever I was stressed or angry, all I wanted to do was get on the court and hit balls. I loved the feeling of a perfect swing, the blood rushing in my ears, the racket hitting the ball. Bounce, thwack! Bounce, thwack! It made me feel as if I was beating up on my enemies or my problems. It took my mind off anything that was bothering me.

If I couldn't hit balls, though, walking with Maddy was the next-best thing. We went out the back door of the clubhouse and crossed the porch, where we could hear the footsteps of the officers on the balcony above. I couldn't help looking around for clues. Maybe one of the idiots who'd done this had dropped a credit card or a personalized cigarette lighter or something. But the porch looked the same as ever, with its old wooden planks, the water fountain against the wall beneath the club bulletin board and the wooden donation box where players put their used balls for the kids' summer camp.

As we walked down the steps of the porch, Maddy's shoulder brushed against a honeysuckle bush. It sent a sweet, summery smell into the air. A few pink buds stayed caught in her long black hair. I couldn't help wondering if they would make her hair smell like flowers too. It probably wasn't the most appropriate thing to wonder at this moment. I looked away. She would think I was a jerk if she caught me staring at her hair like that.

We walked under a long row of trees, along the white-pebble path that led past the tennis courts and the swimming pool to the back of the property. The grass behind the last row of courts sloped down to the banks of the Rideau River. It was 8:00 AM. The courts would normally be filling up with players at this time on a Saturday.

Their emptiness cast a strange silence over everything. It was hard to break that silence. It was hard to think of anything to say.

At the river's edge, a blackbird sang in the cattails. A turtle sunned itself on a rock. Maddy took a seat on a bench overlooking the river, and I sat down next to her. It was the kind of place where a guy could hold a girl's hand. But that probably wasn't the right thing to do under the circumstances either.

Maddy didn't say anything. She just looked down at the path and kicked pebbles with the toes of her sneakers.

"Guess we won't be getting air-conditioning in the clubhouse this summer," I finally said, trying to break the tension with a lame little joke. Every year, the club's board of directors discussed putting AC in the old wooden building. Every year, they decided the club couldn't afford it, and the members had to swelter under the ceiling fans for one more season.

"It's worse than that, Connor." She raised her eyes to look at me from beneath her dark brows. "You have no idea."

Again I felt the urge to take her hand. But how could I? She would probably think I was taking advantage of the situation to come on to her. Only creeps did that kind of thing.

"What's wrong?" I asked.

"The club owes money," she said. "A lot of money."

"A lot?"

She nodded.

"Like...how much?"

"Like, half..." She stopped, as though the words themselves made her gag. Then she spat it out in a rush. "Half a million dollars."

"Half a million?"

She nodded.

"Why?" I asked. "How?"

Maddy stared out over the river. The flower buds still clung to her hair.

"You know the clubhouse is really old, right?" she said.

"Sure." I'd seen the photos of the club when it was built in the 1920s, back when Ottawa was a small town and the club was on the outskirts, almost in the countryside.

"And you know the club's a nonprofit?" she asked.

"Yeah," I said. I even knew what that meant, because my mom worked in charity fundraising. It meant the club was owned by a trust. The money from the membership dues went back into running the tennis programs and the clubhouse, not to some rich owner raking in the dough. The fact that the club was nonprofit was one reason my mom approved of my spending time there, even though she was a crunchy-granola type of person who didn't understand the first thing about tennis.

"We've been members here forever. But my mom only took over as general manager a year ago," Maddy said. "You wouldn't believe it, Connor. The books were in a total mess. There was barely enough money to keep the place running. And there were all these loans that had been taken out over the years to fix things, and they were never paid back. Then we found out the clubhouse needed all kinds of major repairs. The roof, the wiring—

you name it. The club had to take out more loans. It all added up."

I nodded. I understood exactly what she was talking about. My mom and I had the same problems with our house, although I hadn't told Maddy about it. I hadn't told anyone about it.

"Anyway, there's a deadline coming up next month, when we need to put down a big chunk of money on the debt. A hundred thousand bucks," Maddy said. "That's why my mom organized this auction. It was supposed to put the club back on the right track. She's been planning it all year, Connor."

"So what happens now?" I asked.

"You know what happens to people who can't pay the mortgage on their house, right?"

"Yeah. They lose the property," I said. No one needed to tell me that. I knew it from firsthand experience.

"Same thing," said Maddy. "We lose the club."

I followed Maddy's gaze out over the river. A great blue heron rose from the water

17

with heavy wing strokes. Ducks floated among the reeds. There weren't many places like this left in the city. The property must be worth a huge chunk of cash. What would happen if the club was sold at a mortgage-foreclosure auction? Maybe the new owners would turn it into an exclusive private club, for rich kids only. It would become the kind of place I couldn't afford in a million years. Or maybe they would tear it down and build something else. Maybe it wouldn't be a tennis club at all.

"I love this place," said Maddy. "I don't want to lose it."

I wanted to put my arm around her and tell her not to worry, that I would save her club. But that would just be boasting and bragging. We didn't know who had trashed the place. I couldn't even go and punch their lights out, let alone fix the damage they'd done.

My fingers itched for my tennis racket. I wanted the satisfaction of pummeling a serve past a stunned opponent, of whipping a backhand straight down the line. I wanted to get up and fight back, not just sit around watching things fall apart.

On the tennis court, I knew how to fight back.

If only it could be that easy in real life.

chapter three

Three days had passed since the break-in, and the cops hadn't arrested anyone. Everyone was talking about the goons who'd ruined the auction, but no one understood what it really meant for the club. No one except Maddy, her mom and me.

If the members had understood what was going on, there wouldn't have been such a happy, summer-vacation atmosphere at the club. People wouldn't have been laughing and slapping each other on the back and heading up to the porch for drinks after their games. They wouldn't have been acting like the good times at the club were guaranteed to go on forever.

Good times can disappear in a heartbeat. I knew all about that.

It had happened to me a year ago. One night my dad hadn't come home from work. He was a manager at a restaurant, so it was normal for him to work late. But that night he didn't come home at all, and there was no trace of him at the breakfast table the next morning. Later that day, he showed up at my school to take me and my sisters out for lunch and "explain things." He "explained" that he had been having an affair for two years and that he was leaving Mom to go and live with his girlfriend. For two years, the solid ground of my family had been crumbling beneath my feet, and I hadn't even noticed until the moment it all collapsed.

It was like that with the people at the tennis club—they had no idea how unstable the ground was underneath their feet as

21

they served and rallied and called out their scores. They had no idea they could lose it all before the summer was over.

"Serve it up, Connor!" Maddy called from across the court. She bounced lightly on the balls of her feet. Her white tennis skirt swayed against the brown skin of her thighs.

I threw a perfect toss, and I was tempted to wallop the ball full-speed down the T. After all, she was ahead of me 5-4 in our friendly set. But instead, I eased off and sent it to her forehand at about 60 percent power.

I had a secret rule for myself when I played against Maddy—no smoking her with my serves. I hadn't told her about my rule. She would probably be insulted if I did. After all, Maddy was a great player, the top-ranked junior girl in the province. But no girl was used to facing a hundred-mile-an-hour serve. If I creamed her on every serve, we would never get a rally going, and that wouldn't do anything to help my training. Besides, she probably wouldn't want to play against me anymore, and I didn't want that to happen.

Playing tennis was a good way to spend time with Maddy. It was better than going out on a limb and asking her for a date. If she turned me down, I would probably be too embarrassed to ever speak to her again.

Maddy's return came sailing to my forehand. I reamed it down the line into the corner, just beyond the reach of her outstretched racket. 15-0.

Next serve, she drilled the return to my backhand. I slammed it back cross-court, hard and deep to the baseline. We hammered it back and forth until I tried to get fancy and sent a chip shot floating over the net. She sprang forward and finished me off with a sweet smile and a deadly drop shot.

She grinned. "Nice try, Connor."

15-15.

I resisted the temptation to pound her with a monster serve, and Maddy won the next point on an angled forehand with a vicious topspin.

My next serve landed wide and caromed into the court next to ours. Just my luck. It happened to be the court where Rex Hunter was training with his private, two-hundred-dollar-an-hour tennis coach. Rex was the second-ranked junior boy in the province and self-anointed God's Gift to Tennis. I was ranked forty-fifth, about as low as the red clay beneath Rex's feet. And while Rex sauntered around the club showing off his boy-band good looks, I was just an ordinary-looking kid, taller and more athletic than average, but with my fair share of zits and bad-hair days.

Rex paused in his training, ran a hand through his wavy blond hair and casually flipped my ball off the ground with his tennis racket.

"Over here," Maddy called.

Rex turned, beamed his teen-idol smile and tossed the ball to her.

"Thanks!" she said.

I imagined myself at the Donalda Cup Tournament, rubbing Rex's face in the red dirt of the clay courts—metaphorically, of course.

I shook Rex out of my mind and focused on my second serve. I skimmed the ball into the service court like a skipping stone. Maddy's return came back with a spin and bounced low. I smashed it back down the line. But Maddy moved fast, reached the ball and whipped a crosscourt backhand.

The ball came deep and hard. I hit down the line again, but Maddy was already there, anticipating my play. She rifled it crosscourt and I slammed it back, feeling the thrill of matching my strength and wit against hers. For a dozen strokes, she gave as good as she got. Finally, she hit a killer shot that whizzed past my backhand.

15-40. Set point.

Now I really had to beat down the urge to whip my serve at her full-force. Couldn't I bend my rule, just to tie up the game? No, it was better to earn my comeback on a rally, where we faced each other as equals. I went for placement instead of speed, and hit a sweet shot up the middle. It forced her to the backhand. She blocked it. The ball came sailing soft and high over the net, a perfect setup for an overhead smash. I aimed and fired, hammering the ball to her forehand. Somehow, Maddy got there in time and blocked the shot with a diving lunge. I sprang to intercept it at the net. Maddy was overcommitted on her backhand. I dinked it to her forehand. Maddy twisted but couldn't reach it. The ball touched the ground, just wide of the sideline.

"Aargh!" I cried. "Out of bounds! I don't believe it!"

Maddy laughed. "Lucky break for me."

Game and set, Maddy.

She came to meet me at the net, toweling off the sweat from the nape of her neck beneath her black ponytail.

"Good game, Connor," she said. Her smile made losing feel not so bad.

"Want to go upstairs for a soda?" she asked.

I checked my watch. I still had twenty minutes before my shift started at noon. "Sure."

Rex turned to look at us, missing an easy backhand.

"Hunter! Focus!" his coach shouted. I couldn't help smiling. Rex might have the best tennis coach in the city, but I was going for a soda with the only girl at the club who mattered. That was almost as sweet as beating him in straight sets.

We climbed the stairs to the common room. The wreckage from the break-in had been cleared away, but I couldn't help flashing back to the scene in my mind. I could tell by the look on Maddy's face that she was doing the same thing.

"You guys heard anything from the police?" I asked. She shook her head and shrugged. I let it drop.

"How are you getting to the tournament in Toronto this weekend?" she asked.

"Catching a bus," I said. I wasn't looking forward to spending five hours on a cramped, smelly Greyhound, but Mom couldn't afford to take a day off work to drive me.

"We'll give you a lift," said Maddy. "My mom's driving me down."

"Thanks," I said. "I'm staying with my Uncle Phil. In Mississauga."

I tried to sound like Uncle Phil was my best bud, and I'd rather be staying with him in the burbs than in the hotel where everyone else would be rooming. But the fact was, I couldn't afford a hotel room. Almost all the money from my summer job at the club went to pay for equipment and coaching.

"That's no problem," Maddy said. "We can drop you off."

Maddy smiled again, and it spun me off balance, smoked me like a fast drive up the middle. I could barely pull my brains together to mumble, "Thanks."

We got our sodas and took a seat at a table beside the display case full of the club's trophies. It was weird that the vandals hadn't smashed the case, now that I thought about it. You would expect rows of shiny trophies behind glass to be a magnet for thugs.

Of all the trophies in the case, the silver Archibald Cross Memorial Cup shone the brightest. It had recently been polished, in anticipation of the Archibald Cross Memorial Junior Tennis Tournament, scheduled to take place in August.

"You think all those stories are true?" Maddy asked when she saw me looking at the cup.

"Dunno," I said. "I guess we'll find out soon."

Archibald Cross was a self-made million-aire who had joined the club in the 1940s and remained a lifelong member. In his will, he had bequeathed the trophy to the club on the condition that a tournament—the Archibald Cross Memorial Junior Tennis Tournament—be held exactly one year after the day of his death. The junior tennis player who won the tournament would be awarded the cup.

Because old Mr. Cross had been so wealthy, rumors flew that he had hidden something in a secret compartment in the base of the trophy. Some said it was a bar of pure gold. Some said it was a check for a million dollars. Some said it was the first nickel he had ever earned, working as a shoeshine boy in the Dirty Thirties.

"I could definitely use the money," I said.

"Yeah," said Maddy. "Me too."

I felt a pang of embarrassment, because I knew Maddy would give the money to her mom to pay the club's debt. Meanwhile, I'd been thinking of all the ways I could use the money to further my own tennis career—hire elite coaches, sign up for winter training camps in Florida, fly to international tournaments and buy all the things I needed to give me an edge against the preppy rich kids like Rex who dominated the tennis circuit.

I checked my watch. It was 11:50, and I still needed a shower. I couldn't be late for my shift, or I'd catch it from Maddy's mom. I finished my soda and got up. But before I left the common room, I took one last glance at the gleaming silver Archibald Cross Memorial Cup.

Suddenly I wanted it more than any other prize I had ever played for. And it wasn't for the glory of the cup. It was for the money I imagined might be stashed inside.

Money wasn't something I had thought about much as a kid. But I was sixteen now, and some of life's realities were starting to hit me. I couldn't help thinking that a stack of dough would solve a whole lot of problems.

chapter four

After two subway transfers and a bus ride from Uncle Phil's place in Mississauga, I arrived for the Toronto tournament at the posh Donalda Club. Manicured lawns, leather furniture, granite hallways—that about summed up the Donalda Club. It was a long way from the homey atmosphere of the Bytowne Tennis Club back in Ottawa. It was an even longer way from the rundown bungalow where I lived with my mom and my sisters.

I felt antsy from being cooped up in public transit too long. I couldn't wait to hit a few balls and loosen up my muscles before my first game. The woman at the reception desk pointed the way to the locker room and to my assigned practice court. The sun was shining, and the temperature was in the low twenties. I was feeling good about the day.

The U16 tournament at the Donalda had a four-star ranking, which meant the best kids in the province would be competing. It also meant that if I finished high, I would earn a bunch of points to bump up my provincial ranking. That was important because the Donalda was my last chance to get my ranking into the top thirty-two provincially, which would qualify me to play in the Ontario finals at the end of July.

If I ranked in the top eight at the provincials, I would earn a spot in the national championships in August, which was my real goal. All the scouts from the big American colleges would be hanging out at the nationals, trying to spot talent.

If I impressed a scout, I could win a scholarship to a US school. Then I would be able to play on the American college circuit, hopefully score some big wins and even find a corporate sponsor. It was the best route for a kid like me, who didn't have a lot of money, to turn pro.

On the other hand, if I failed to get to the nationals, I'd probably end up studying to be a plumber at some small-time college in Canada that didn't even have a tennis team.

Getting into the top thirty-two was a big jump from my current ranking of forty-fifth. But I believed I could make it. I didn't think my ranking reflected my true ability. A lot of the kids had been competing since they were seven or eight years old. They had reached the top of their game and were starting to plateau. Me, I'd grown up playing a bunch of sports—soccer, basketball, volleyball, track and field. I'd played pretty much anything my school or the local community center offered to keep me off the streets while my parents were at work.

I'd picked up a tennis racket for the first time at thirteen. At first the wonky scoring system threw me for a loop. For some strange reason, zero is called "love." From there the points go fifteen, thirty, forty, game. If the players are tied at forty, it's called "deuce," and you need to score two more consecutive points to win the game. The first player to win six games takes the set, but you have to win by a margin of two games. Two out of three sets wins the match.

After I got used to the weirdness of the scoring system, I found out I loved tennis. From fourteen on, it was all I wanted to play. As far as I was concerned, my game was on the rise. I was on a steep learning curve, and I intended to blow past my competitors.

Especially Rex.

I spent an hour hitting practice balls, then showered and showed up for my first game at 1:00 PM. My opponent was a skinny fifteen-year-old who hadn't had his growth spurt yet. He looked like he desperately wanted to be back in the U14 category. I hammered him with my serves until he gave up trying to return them. Whenever he served, I hit the returns hard down the line. Same shot every time. I pummeled him 6-1, 6-0. The kid never stood a chance.

In the second round, I was matched to a hulking sixteen-year-old with a powerful serve, but no speed in his feet. Wielding the racket in his meaty hand, he looked like a linebacker on vacation at summer tennis camp. I responded to his serves by sticking my racket into the path of the ball and hoping it rebounded somewhere on his side of the net. Technically, it's called a "block." I called it my deflector shield. If I could just get the ball into play, I knew I could beat him on the rally by making him run. He took the first set, started to tire by the second and was wheezing by the third. 4-6, 6-4, 6-2. My victory.

That evening, I sat for an hour in Uncle Phil's hot tub, drank three quarts of Gatorade and rubbed all my muscles down with A535. I was sore. But I had no joint pain and no injuries. I was in good form for the next day's quarterfinals.

I arrived early that morning, signed in and got started on my warm-up. I needed to loosen up and calm my nerves, because I knew the competition was about to get a lot tougher. The kid I faced in the quarter-finals was Bruno Chan. Bruno was ranked fifteenth in the province. He was known for his lightning speed. No matter where you put the ball, Bruno would get a racket on it. That was his biggest strength. Bruno's biggest weakness was his lack of accuracy. Too often his shots bounced long or wide, giving his opponent points on unforced errors. I knew I needed to collect those points to win the game.

I arrived at my court a few minutes before game time and looked around to see if Maddy might have come by to watch me. She wasn't there, but I spotted Rex hanging around with his coach.

At 10:00 AM, the match started. For the first couple of games, I kept trying to sneak the ball past Bruno. I would put it right down the line, or crosscourt in the far corner where I thought he couldn't reach it. But those lightning-fast feet lived up to their reputation. Worse, I kept hitting balls outside the line, because I was trying too hard to score a winner. Midway through the first set, with the score a miserable 0-3 in Bruno's favor, I realized that if I wanted to win, I had to stop giving away points against myself.

From then on, I stuck to what I was good at—big serves and hard hits from the baseline. I drove the ball into his court with all my force and waited for him to make a mistake. I soon found that the harder I hit it, the more often Bruno's returns went flying out of bounds. I couldn't recover from my deficit on the first set. But I won the next two, 6-4 and 6-3. Bruno looked surprised to be overturned by a kid ranked so far below him. But he shook my hand like a good sport.

The semifinal match lay ahead of me. My opponent, Rex Hunter.

We shook hands before the match and wished each other a good game. We were supposed to be pals, I guess, since we belonged to the same club. But I didn't feel any loyalty to Rex. He'd been a member at our crosstown rival, the Rideau Tennis Club, since he was a little kid. He'd only switched to our club this year, after his family moved into a brand-new condo in the neighborhood. They wanted to support their local club, his dad said, as if they were doing us all a big favor by gracing us with their presence.

I won the toss and took the first serve. High on my toes, I smashed the ball over the net. *Blew it right by him,* I thought. But no, the ball came winging back, catching me off guard. I hit a defensive return. Rex charged the net and finessed a drop shot that pitter-patted into the forecourt. I dove to reach it but couldn't get there in time. 0-15.

That shook my concentration, and I hit my next serve into the net. Second serve, I took it easy. Hit a nice, safe, soft one that Rex sent zinging deep to my backhand. I got a racket on it but netted the ball. 0-30.

How could it be love-30 when I was pouring my heart into every shot, and Rex was lounging there at the baseline, grinning as though he was humoring me by even picking up his racket? I gritted my teeth and blasted my hardest serve at him. It must have clocked in at 120 MPH. Rex sent it back, deep. Fine. I could play the baseline. That was my kind of game. I whipped it back crosscourt. Rex went down the line. I tried for crosscourt, but the ball bounced midcourt instead. Easy hit for Rex. He sent me running to the opposite corner. I got there but didn't have time to make a good shot. I hit it back to the midcourt. Too easy. Rex finished me off with a surgical strike to the far corner. 0-40. Triple break point.

I forced myself to take a deep breath. Refocus. I wished I had some kind of trick serve up my sleeve. But all I knew how to do was hit with all my might. So that's what I did. Rex returned with a block shot. I hit it deep. He sliced it back. The ball bounced low, with a ton of spin. I dug it out and sent it high. It was a perfect overhead setup for Rex. He smashed it into the far corner. Game.

Rex had broken me on the very first game.

Welcome to the next level of competition, Connor. Think you can take it?

Second game, it was Rex's turn to serve. The ball came at me fast, but not too fast. I decided to play it safe. I hit a good, hard return, nothing fancy. Too late, I looked up and saw that Rex had charged to the forecourt. My ball had barely cleared the net when he returned it with a volley at a sharp angle that even lightning-fast Bruno Chan couldn't have reached. 15-0.

Serve and volley? Serve and volley went out in the 1990s. No one played serve and volley anymore.

Correction. Rex played serve and volley. He played it like he was on fire.

The match went on like that. I blasted my hardest shots at him. Rex flitted around the court like it was his personal dance floor, hitting volleys, drop shots, dinks and slices. He had all the moves, and he was having a blast. I felt like a puny little kid trying to beat up on his big brother.

When the smoke cleared, Rex had given me a whipping. I'd lost the first set 6-2 and the second set a miserable 6-1.

Rex advanced to the finals. But I didn't stay to watch him play. Instead, I slunk back to the Greyhound station for the long bus ride home.

That night, I checked the results on the Internet. In the top spot, in bold type, stood the name of the new number-one kid in the province—Rex Hunter. I had to scroll way down to find my name—Connor Trent, ranked thirtieth.

I should have been happy. I'd made the top thirty-two and qualified for the provincial championships. I tried to tell myself that I had achieved my goal for the weekend. But I knew I was still miles away from beating Rex.

chapter five

It was 6:00 AM the Monday after the Donalda tournament. I'd just finished the four-mile run from my house to the tennis club, and I was planning on grabbing the ball machine from the equipment room for an hour of practice before my shift started at seven. But as I entered the club, dripping with sweat, a noise from Mrs. Sharma's office made me poke my head inside. Maddy was sitting at her mom's desk, watching the security video from the night of the break-in.

"Hey, Connor. Look at this," she said.

I came closer, but not too close. I didn't want to drip sweat all over her.

"What about it?" I asked. I didn't see anything different from the first time we had watched it—five guys in ski masks, swaggering across the little parking area in front of the club. They reached the chain-link fence, had some kind of a discussion, then one guy jumped on the fence and the others followed. They climbed over, and that's where the security camera lost them.

"Look," Maddy said. She rewound the video to where the guys were crossing the parking lot. "Look at the kid at the back, on the left."

The guy was chubbier than the others, and now that she'd pointed him out, I could see that his walk was different too. He ambled along with a sort of lilt to his steps.

"He's walking funny," I said.

She nodded. "Yeah. And look what he's wearing."

I squinted at the TV. The video was blurry, so it was hard to make out details.

"Is that a Mickey Mouse sweatshirt?"
Weird, I thought.

"Yeah," said Maddy. "I think I know that kid."

"Seriously?" I reached for the phone to call the cops, but Maddy stopped me.

"Hang on. I want to talk to him first."

"Why?"

"Quinte's a little...different."

"So what?"

"You'll see when you meet him. Just trust me, okay?"

The house Maddy took me to that afternoon was a droopy little bungalow half a block down from the nice two-storey brick house where Maddy and her family lived. The street was in an older neighborhood where lots of people had renovated their houses to make them bigger and swankier, adding things like sun decks or stone landscaping. Some houses had even been knocked down and replaced with tall, boxy duplexes squashed into tiny yards. But every

45

once in a while, you found a house like this one. It was a sad little house, left behind by its neighbors, with peeling paint and a sagging front porch.

Even though I still wanted to nail this Quinte kid, whoever he was, I felt bad for him when I saw his house. It reminded me of the place my sisters and I had been living in since Dad and Mom split up last year—a fixer-upper that never really got fixed up, a broken-down house with a broken-down family inside it. Maybe there was something broken inside Quinte's house too.

Maddy rang the bell and a woman answered it. I smelled hamburgers cooking. A TV blared somewhere in the background.

"Hi, Mrs. McFarlane. This is my friend Connor. We were just heading to my place, and I thought I'd drop by to say hi to Quinte."

Maddy beamed a smile at her. You'd never know we were going to question her son on suspicion of vandalism.

"That's so sweet of you, Madhavi," Mrs. McFarlane said. "He's in the basement. Go on down."

In the basement rec room, a chubby teenage kid was sitting on the sofa, playing a video game. He was wearing a Mickey Mouse sweatshirt. I shot a look at Maddy. She nodded and sat down next to Quinte. I stayed standing. I didn't want to act like I was the guy's pal or anything, not if I was going to rat him out to the cops.

"Hi, Quinte," said Maddy.

"I'm smashing aliens," said Quinte. He didn't look at her. On the TV screen, a video-game caveman was hitting little green creatures with an enormous club. More creatures were parachuting down from a spaceship, which was shooting laser beams at the caveman. Quinte was really getting a kick out of it, shouting sound effects as he whacked the aliens with his caveman avatar.

"Can I play?" asked Maddy.

"No. It's the rule. Only one player," said Quinte.

The spaceship sent out a beam of purple light, which frazzled the caveman into a pile of digital dust. A message flashed on the screen. THE ALIENS HAVE CONQUERED!

"No fair!" Quinte complained. "You ruined my game."

"Sorry, Quinte," said Maddy. "This is my friend Connor."

Quinte looked up at me, but not really *at* me. His eyes were focused somewhere about six inches to the left of my head. Maddy was right—Quinte was a different kind of kid. He was not all there, or something.

"I smashed four hundred and ninety-eight aliens," he said. "When you smash five hundred, you get a bigger club."

"Yeah?" I said.

"You get a bigger club if you smash five hundred aliens," Quinte continued, "and if you smash a thousand, you get a rocket launcher!"

"Cool. I love to smash stuff," said Maddy. "Smashing stuff's cool—right, Connor?"

"Yeah, really cool," I said. I wasn't sure where she was going with this.

"Did you see Baghdatis at the Australian Open?" Maddy went on. "He smashed four

rackets in a row. Totally mangled them."
She laughed, as though destroying a two-
hundred-dollar racket was the funniest thing
in the world. "It was awesome."

Quinte got a gleam in his eye. "I smashed
a tennis racket," he said.

Maddy shot a look at me. Now I understood what she was doing. It was too easy
to trap this kid.

"Smashing rackets is cool," said Maddy.
"I love smashing rackets."

"Yeah, but you're not allowed to tell,"
Quinte said. "It's a secret."

"Who says it's a secret?" said Maddy.

"The other guys. I got fifty bucks. Fifty
bucks!"

"What other guys?" I asked. But Quinte
drew back, as though he didn't trust me
to keep his secret. He picked up the video
console and started smashing aliens again.

Maddy tried to talk to him some more.
But she couldn't get him back on the topic
of the tennis racket. He just kept talking
about aliens and the type of weaponry used

to smash them. Finally, we left. Maddy called goodbye to Mrs. McFarlane as we let ourselves out the front door.

"He's guilty," I said when the door closed behind us.

"That's pretty obvious," said Maddy. She started walking away from the little house and past the houses of the richer neighbors, with their well-kept lawns and big, shady maple trees. I kept pace beside her.

"So let's call the cops," I said.

"Nice, Connor. Throw him to the wolves," said Maddy. "You know he's not right in the head."

"What else are we supposed to do?"

"I don't know, Connor. Maybe...I don't know."

She sat down on the curb and started fiddling with a twig she'd picked up from the sidewalk. "What about those other kids on the video?" she said finally. "I bet they put him up to it. He said he got fifty bucks."

"Fifty bucks to smash things. That must've been his idea of heaven." I sat down next to her.

"Connor!"

"It's true. Besides, it doesn't even make any sense. Why would they pay him fifty bucks to smash things?"

Maddy shrugged. "Maybe he didn't want to, and they paid him to go along with it."

"Didn't want to smash things? Are you kidding?" I asked.

"Yeah, you're right," Maddy said.

"And besides, why pay him to trash the club? I mean, I could understand if they paid him fifty bucks to steal a stereo or something. But trashing a tennis auction? What's in it for them?"

Maddy shrugged. "I don't know."

"I still say we turn him in to the cops."

Maddy fiddled with her stick some more, drawing doodles in the loose dirt on the sidewalk.

"I wish we knew who those other kids were," said Maddy.

"Maybe he'll rat them out."

"Yeah, and maybe he won't. And maybe he'll go to jail. Did you think about that?"

"Okay," I said. "But what about the club?"

"How's ratting out Quinte going to help the club?"

"You could sue him."

"Yeah, like he's got any money, Connor."

I couldn't think of an answer to that. So I sat there awkwardly, saying nothing. I hated the feeling of arguing with her. I wanted her to know I wasn't mad at her. I was mad at the guys who had vandalized the club and put it on the brink of bankruptcy. For what? Cheap kicks?

"I don't know what we're going to do, Connor," said Maddy. "But I know we can't just lay it all on Quinte. We've been neighbors since forever. We used to play together when we were little kids. My parents are friends with his parents. They come over to our place for barbecues, for God's sake. I can't just rat him out. How would I face his family?"

She looked at me with her chin in her hands, her face cupped in her long, slender fingers, and her dark hair falling around her shoulders.

"Okay," I said. "We'll think of something else."

But I didn't know what else we would think of, if we threw away our prime suspect.

I wished I knew who had given Quinte fifty bucks. I wished I could figure out why. I thought back to the question one of the cops had asked the day we'd discovered the vandalism.

Do you know anyone who would want to target the club?

chapter six

As though I didn't have enough problems, my mom was on a crusade. It was her first crusade since the divorce, and she was really throwing herself into it.

I had seen Mom on crusades before, so I knew what to expect. The fridge could be empty for weeks. Rats could be dancing the macarena on the living room sofa. And Mom would be on the phone, giving heck to some city official, blind to the chaos around her.

At the moment, Mom was on a crusade to save the Tree.

The Tree was a gigantic oak growing on the huge front lawn of a little, old house at the end of our street. When I say gigantic, I mean gigantic. It was so big, if two people stood on either side of it and tried to reach their arms around the trunk, they wouldn't be able to touch each other's fingers.

The little, old house had been owned by a little, old woman who used to come out and sit under the oak tree and watch the world go by. But the woman had died, and her kids had sold the property to a developer. The developer wanted to cut down the oak, knock down the house and build condos on the property.

Mom was on a crusade to stop him.

So when I got home that evening after my encounter with Quinte, I wasn't surprised to find the fridge empty and my mom at the kitchen table, half-buried in a pile of reports and reference papers. I was lucky there were no rats partying on the sofa.

"Fish sticks in the freezer. Sorry, I didn't get around to shopping today," said Mom, barely looking up.

"Where are Cyn and Tara?" I asked. I didn't see any sign of my sisters.

"Babysitting. You're on your own for dinner," Mom said. "I have to go to a meeting tonight."

I could figure out what the meeting was about by the report in her hand, titled "Preserving the Urban Treescape—An Analysis of Municipal Green-Space Policy."

"Mom, I thought we were painting tonight," I said. "The real estate agent's coming tomorrow. Remember?"

"I forgot. Don't worry—I'll call her and put her off till next week."

"But Mom, the house really needs a paint job."

"Connor." Mom lowered her reading glasses and looked at me. "This house gives me a royal pain in the butt. I have no intention of spending the night painting it when I have more important things on my hands."

"Like saving the Tree," I grumbled.

"Yes." She stared at me. "Like saving the Tree."

Mom started gathering up her papers and shoving them into a file folder.

The house gave me a royal pain in the butt, too, mainly because it was the result of my parents' divorce, which was the rottenest thing that had happened in my life.

After Dad left, Mom got half the money from the sale of our old house. She used it to buy this house, which she got for a "good price" because it was a "fixer-upper." But after we moved in, we found out the house needed way more "fixing-upping" than the real estate agent had told us about. The plumbing, the wiring and the foundation all needed work. Pretty soon the money was gone, and Mom still owed a huge mortgage. It was one of those weird mortgages where you pay basically nothing for the first year, and after that the monthly payments jump into the stratosphere. Mom couldn't afford the payments, and now we had to sell the house—fast.

I was no real-estate whiz. But even I could figure out that we would get more money for the house if we painted it. Try telling that to Mom, though, when she was on a crusade.

"Mom, we need the money…"

"Connor," she snapped. "Do not lecture me about money. I am perfectly capable of supporting my family. I have a job. We are not going to starve. We are not going to be living in a cardboard box on the streets. It's not going to kill us to rent an apartment for a while. Frankly, I couldn't care less if this bloody house fell down around my ears. But that Tree out there"—she pointed at the window—"*that* is worth saving."

"Fine," I said. "I'm painting."

I stomped out of the kitchen, grabbed a can of paint from the front hall and took it into the living room. The walls were a hideous shade of pastel purple. Mom said the color had been trendy in the 1980s.

I jacked open the can and started slapping paint on the wall. I heard Mom let herself out the front door, but I didn't call goodbye. I didn't know why I was so angry all of a sudden. Maybe I was mad about losing my house. Maybe I was mad about losing my dad. Maybe I was still mad about losing to Rex at the Donalda or mad about losing my club to a bunch of idiots who got their kicks destroying other people's property. Maybe I was just tired of being a loser all the time. Maybe I was sick of comparing myself to Rex. Rex, the top-ranked junior in the province. Rex, whose dad was a hotshot businessman. Rex the winner. Connor the loser.

Sometimes, when I was hitting practice balls at the club in the early morning when no one else was there, I would fantasize about going all the way. I would dream of winning the provincials, winning the nationals and hitting the international junior circuit.

But playing international tennis costs a truckload of money. With coaches, equipment, airfares, hotels and meals, you had to figure about a hundred grand a year in expenses. And juniors didn't win any money in tournaments. No one won cash until they turned pro.

Tennis was for rich boys like Rex, I told myself as I slopped the thick white paint over the sickly purple wall. Why did I even think I could compete?

Mom got home at around eleven o'clock and flopped down on the living room sofa. I was up on a ladder, finishing the last corner of the room.

"This looks great, honey. Thanks," she said. "I'm sorry I got mad at you earlier."

"That's okay." I ran the brush down the corner angle. "How'd the meeting go?"

"Great. There's lots of community support. The head of the neighborhood association is on side. He's going to bring an application to have it designated a heritage tree. Of course, the mayor's in the pocket of the developers. But I'm optimistic."

"That's good, Mom," I said. I finished painting the corner, came down from the ladder and sat on the floor next to her.

"One day, I'll be a pro tennis player and we won't have to worry about money anymore," I said.

She smiled. "It's good to have a dream, honey. But let's keep saving for college, just in case."

"Sure, Mom."

I didn't tell her about my plan to win a tennis scholarship to an American college. She would think it was impossible. She wouldn't believe anyone would pay a kid's college tuition just because he could whack a ball with a racket. To her, there were more important things in life than sports. To her, saving a single oak tree on a tiny street that no one had ever heard of was worth a hundred times more than winning the trophy at world-famous Wimbledon.

I took the brushes to the sink and cleaned them. Then I hit the sack. I had to be up at five the next morning to train for the provincials.

chapter seven

The provincial championships were coming up in two weeks' time, and even though I had other things on my mind, I needed to focus on getting ready. Going in, I would be one of the lowest-ranked players. I would need to pull off some major upsets to make it into the top eight and qualify for the junior nationals.

I started training harder than ever, adding push-ups, sit-ups, bench presses and Russian twists to my workout. I ran up and down hills. I practiced sprinting and stopping, exploding from a standstill into full-speed action. I played practice matches as often as I could, with Maddy and anyone else who would take me on. I spent my paycheck on extra lessons from Armand, the club pro.

The vandalism at the club still bugged me though. In training, I could take my mind off it. But afterward, as soon as I got into the hot shower or on the jog home, I would wonder about the other guys on the surveillance video. Who were they? What was their deal?

I had a couple of mornings off work that week, so I decided to follow Quinte around and see which kids he hung out with. It was easy to pretend I was out jogging while I spied on him.

Maddy had told me that Quinte went to a special school. They had small classes for kids they called "developmentally delayed." The school also had classes for kids who had nothing wrong with their brains— they just had bad attitudes. They were the kids who got kicked out of regular school because the teachers couldn't control them. It was a group of those kids that Quinte hung out with.

They were mean. They picked on Quinte, but he didn't realize it. It was as if they kept him around just to make fun of him.

One day, I saw them goad Quinte into throwing a lit match into a Dumpster in the alley behind a Chinese food restaurant. When the restaurant owner ran out, shouting and waving a fire extinguisher, the other kids took off. Quinte was left standing there with a clueless grin on his face, probably thinking he had torched a bunch of Dumpster-dwelling aliens. Luckily for him, the restaurant owner didn't call the police. He was too busy putting out the fire.

Another day, the same kids got Quinte to shoplift a gold chain from a jewelry store. Quinte was so klutzy, the burly security guard caught him before he got to the door. "Nice try, kid," he said, flinging Quinte outside.

The other guys, watching from around the corner, laughed when they saw him fly across the sidewalk and land facedown on the hood of a parked car.

I didn't have any hard evidence, but it was pretty obvious to me that these kids were the same ones who had trashed our club.

The only thing that stopped me from going straight to the cops was knowing Maddy would be against it. We couldn't rat out the other kids without also ratting out Quinte. Maddy would never agree to that. And although I hated to admit it, she had a point. Quinte obviously didn't understand what was going on. He would do anything to please his so-called friends.

One of the kids looked really familiar, but I didn't figure out who he was until the third day, when I spotted him wearing a Rideau Tennis Club T-shirt. Then it clicked. His name was Mike Baron, and he was a tennis player who trained at Rideau Club. I had faced him before in tournaments.

If Mike Baron was one of the guys who had trashed our club, things might make sense. Maybe it wasn't a random act of vandalism. Maybe it was Mike's dirty way of striking a blow against his crosstown rival.

I jogged back to the club, eager to tell Maddy what I'd found out. I was hoping to catch her alone, but when I arrived she was crammed into the small office with her mom, Rex and Rex's dad. She was updating the club's website with a picture of Rex hoisting the silver Donalda Club Tournament trophy over his head.

"Put it right at the top of the page, Madhavi," her mother said as I squeezed into the office. "It's not every day one of our members wins the Donalda."

"Top of the province!" said Mr. Hunter, thumping Rex on the shoulder. Rex smiled. He looked his usual preppy self, in a pale yellow Lacoste tennis shirt. His dad was wearing a business suit and gold cuff links. Cuff links! I thought those went out with the serve and volley.

Mrs. Sharma turned toward me as I approached.

"Oh, hello, Connor," she said. "Connor did quite well at the tournament too. Didn't you?"

"I made the provincials," I said, trying not to sound boastful or bitter about Rex.

"Great stuff!" Mr. Hunter boomed. "I saw your semifinal match against Rex. What a drubbing!"

I shut my mouth because I didn't want to appear unsportsmanlike. Who used the word *drubbing* anymore, anyway?

"Guess I'll see you at the provincials, then," said Rex.

"Yeah," I said. With any luck, I'd make him eat my dust.

"Oh, Madhavi," Mrs. Sharma broke in. "We have to put something up on the website about the black-tie fundraiser."

"Yeah, just a sec," said Maddy.

While she fiddled with the website, her mom explained her new idea for generating the money she'd hoped to raise at the tennis auction. It was going to be a high-class thing with men in tuxes and women in long gowns, cocktails served at the bar and live music by a jazz quartet. It didn't sound like anything I would go to in a million years.

"A black-tie event? Sounds like fun," said Mr. Hunter. "Who's your celebrity guest?"

"Uh..." Mrs. Sharma hesitated. "Well, the deputy mayor is a member. And I thought we'd ask the host of the HOT 89.9 morning show—"

"No, no, you need an A-list celebrity," Rex's dad said. "You need...let me think..." He tapped his fingers on his chin, then flicked his index at her. "You need Alanis Morissette."

"Alanis Morissette?" Mrs. Sharma sounded stunned, as though Mr. Hunter had suggested we ring up Justin Bieber and ask him to drop by and play a little gig between his million-dollar engagements.

"Sure. Nice girl. Known her family for ages," Mr. Hunter said. "She's in town this summer. Laying low at her family's cottage on the lake."

"Can you get her?" Mrs. Sharma's voice was a mixture of hope and doubt.

"Sure. She won't want a big production though. How about an intimate acoustic concert? A couple hundred people? At a hundred dollars a ticket?"

"Sounds wonderful," Mrs. Sharma said. "We could set up a stage by the pool. We'll put out floating candles, patio lanterns."

"I'll get right on it," Mr. Hunter said. He turned to his son. "You'll get the younger generation on board, Rex?"

"Sure thing, Dad," said Rex. "It'll be like a retro-nineties thing."

Mr. Hunter looked at his watch. "Well, gotta get back to the office," he said. In a flash of gold cuff links he was gone, leaving Mrs. Sharma to chatter on about how marvelous he was, and what a great bene-factor to the club.

Maddy finished working on the website, unplugged a camera from the computer and handed it back to Rex.

"Thanks." Rex flashed a smile at her. "Hey, I know you're working, but it's lunch-time. Want to take a spin on my Harley?"

"Cool," said Maddy. She glanced at me but then looked away so quickly, I wasn't sure what to read into it. "Can I go, Mom?"

"I need you back in half an hour," Mrs. Sharma said.

She smiled while Maddy and Rex went out the door together, but I just stood there, feeling sucker-punched. I had hoped to impress Maddy with my detective work. Instead, she was going off with Rex.

"I thought you weren't working until this evening, Connor," Mrs. Sharma said.

"Yeah, I came to get the ball machine," I said.

For the next two hours, the machine whipped balls at me, and I slammed them back as though I were slamming them into Rex Hunter's face.

chapter eight

Two days before the U16 championships, my mom broke the news that she couldn't drive me to Toronto. Her fight to save the Tree wasn't going well, so she was ramping up her plan of action. She was going to hold a sit-in.

When I got up at 5:00 AM Friday to catch the 6:00 AM Greyhound, the only sign of Mom was a note on the kitchen table wishing me good luck beside a brown-bag breakfast of muffins and fruit. I guzzled some OJ, mowed down a couple of muffins and headed for the bus station.

The street was empty except for the squirrels—until I came to the big corner lot where the Tree stood. There, sitting in a fork of the massive trunk, was my mother. She was wearing a navy-blue tracksuit, drinking tea from a thermos and reading a report titled "Guidelines for Planning Sustainable Neighborhoods."

"Good luck, Connor!" Mom waved.

"Thanks, Mom," I muttered.

At least I'd be getting out of town before the entire street woke up and discovered my mother perched in the Tree like the Lorax, except less cute and fuzzy.

I got off the Greyhound in suburban Toronto and took a city bus to the Ontario Racquet Club. It was a far cry from the Donalda. The club had about the same level of elegance as your average Walmart store. But what it lacked in ritziness, it made up for in size. The echoing concrete hallways stretched for miles, branching off into massive gyms where rows of sweaty people worked out on exercise machines. Outside, acres of tennis courts lay splayed under the baking sun.

I played my first elimination round on Friday afternoon. It was a tough match that went to three sets and left me dripping with sweat and tasting salt every time I licked my lips. I beat my opponent, though, and then I checked the board to see which player I would face in the second elimination round, on Saturday morning.

The name I saw made me burn.

It was Mike Baron.

Mike had a fighting look in his eye and a cocky sneer on his lips when I met him in the locker room the next morning before our match.

"You trashed my club. I'm gonna trash you," I said.

"Fat chance, loser," Mike snarled back.

Out on the court, Mike played my style of tennis. He hit big, hard serves and power strokes from the baseline. He was a tough kid, full of grit and anger.

We played long, grinding rallies, driving the ball at each other full-force, grunting like animals, with the sweat flying off our faces and the hot, smoggy air burning our lungs. It was hand-to-hand combat, down in the trenches, fighting for every inch of ground. When we came up for air, we were tied 6-6 in the first set. Neither of us had broken the other's serve. Neither was anywhere near conceding defeat.

We traded points in a grueling tiebreaker, then Mike took the lead at 12-11, with my turn to serve. I went on the attack with a monster serve that should have left Mike reeling, but he stuck out his racket for a block shot and put the ball in play. Another jaw-clenching rally followed. With every hit, I imagined ramming the ball down Mike's throat. We stayed deadlocked for eight hits, ten hits, twelve hits, until finally he powered it past me for the point and won the tiebreaker 13-11.

We both knew it could have gone either way. We both knew that we would grind each other into the ground before one of us came out victorious.

The next set was a replay of the first, except this time I came out on top, half through luck and half through stubborn bloody-mindedness. Now we stood tied at one set apiece. On the break before the third set, I sat in my courtside chair, guzzling water, feeling the burning in my lungs and my legs and wondering how I would dig deep enough to win the final bout against Mike.

Then someone called my name. I looked around and saw Maddy's face pressed up against the fence.

"Let's go, Connor!" she shouted.

The sight of her sent a jolt of energy through my body. What was she doing here? What was she doing watching me? Wasn't Rex playing an elimination match on some other court? Wouldn't she rather be watching him, the winner of the Donalda tournament, the top-ranked junior in the province?

I waved at Maddy, then jerked my thumb across the net toward Mike. Earlier in the week, I'd filled her in on my suspicions about him.

She nodded. "Cream him, Connor! Take him down!"

Take him down. Yeah, I'd take him down, for Maddy's sake *and* to get justice for what he'd done to my club.

I opened the final set with a screaming serve. Then I followed up with a series of punishing forehands that Mike beat back with grim aggression. On and on we fought as the scorching sun inched toward its high point in the noonday sky. I felt the burning in my skin, muscles, throat and lungs. Every point was a battle, and we held each other in a death grip, each of us straining to bring the other down. In between points, I looked at Maddy, her fingers gripping the chain-link fence, and energy surged through me again.

At last we were tied at four games apiece on the final set. Mike was serving. The score stood at deuce when Mike double-faulted, giving me the advantage. Break point. It was my chance to pull ahead.

Mike served. I blocked it back. He hit a whopper to my backhand. I returned it crosscourt. He blasted it to my backhand. I slammed it down the line. This wouldn't be just another brutal baseline rally, I decided. This time, I was watching for an opportunity to surprise him. We exchanged blows twice more, and then I blasted the ball crosscourt to the corner. Mike reached it, but just barely. Here was my chance. I rushed the net. The ball soared toward me. I gave it a touch of underspin and dropped it dead into Mike's forecourt. He pivoted, lunged, but he was too far away to reach it. The ball dribbled away, so soft and yet so deadly. Game, Connor.

Maddy whistled. Mike slammed his racket on the ground. It was 5-4, and I was up a break. All I had to do now was hold serve to take the match.

I faulted on my first serve out of sheer nervousness but whipped a hard second serve to Mike's backhand. He hammered it back, hard and deep. Another baseline rally began. But things had changed. I had shown him I was willing to take a risk. I had a feeling he might be willing to take a risk too.

I tried to keep him back at the baseline, but I could see he was trying to come up. He was cheating a few steps forward, looking for his chance to rush the net. Finally, he did. He tried a drop volley like I had played on him, but he couldn't finesse it. He got too much power on the shot, and it landed midcourt. I scooped it up and sent it to an unprotected back corner. 15-0. Mike was seeing blood.

I sent a monster serve caroming at him, and he hit it back, out of bounds. Maddy let out a holler like a wild jungle girl. 30-0. Mike took the next point on a jet-powered return. I took the next one with an ace up the middle. 40-15. Match point.

At the baseline, I took a deep breath and gave the ball a few bounces, getting ready to serve. I watched it hit the ground next to the tip of my white tennis sneaker. I felt the sun blaze on the back of my neck. Blood pounded in my ears. I tossed the ball with my left hand and swung my right in a synchronized arc. My racket hit the ball at the top of the arc. I felt my arm come sweeping down on the follow-through. I saw Mike moving to block it. I knew the return was coming crosscourt. I felt my legs moving to the spot. I heard the perfect thwack of the ball. I felt it hitting my racket on the sweet spot. I saw it speeding down the line, and I saw Mike running for it. I saw his return come sailing at me, and I knew my next shot would go crosscourt to the opposite corner. I hit it there with the precision of a hawk striking its prey, and I was ready for Mike's return. But it never came. Mike never reached the ball.

Game, set, match. Somehow I staggered through the motions of a handshake. Somehow I stumbled off the court and into the arms of Maddy, who hugged me around the neck, laughing and jumping up and down. I held her tightly around her slim waist, thinking I had walked into a miracle—the miracle of beating Mike, the miracle of holding this girl in my arms.

I only needed one more miracle today—the miracle of a win in the quarterfinals against Rex Hunter.

chapter nine

Sometimes miracles don't happen, especially when they involve a dead-tired underdog beating the top-ranked guy in the province. That afternoon, Rex wiped the floor with me.

He took me in straight sets, his dad shouting and grinning like a fool from the sidelines. Even Maddy clapped when he won. I knew she had to because her mom was there and Rex was a member of our club. Still, it felt like a betrayal.

Maddy and her mom invited me out for dinner that night, along with Rex and his dad. It was an all-you-can-eat spaghetti place, and Mrs. Sharma kept piling my plate with noodles, insisting that I needed to rebuild my strength. I didn't mind. As long I was stuffing my face, I didn't have to make conversation with Rex and his obnoxious dad. It burned me, though, to listen to Rex and Maddy swapping thoughts on the upcoming semifinals, which I wouldn't be playing in.

After dinner, Mrs. Sharma drove me to the bus station. She and Maddy were staying to watch the rest of the tournament, but I didn't have the heart to sit in the bleachers and pretend to cheer for Rex. Maddy gave me a hug before I boarded the bus. I tried to keep the feeling of it in my mind during the long, dreary ride home.

Making the quarterfinals was a good result, I reminded myself. Best of all, it guaranteed me a spot at the nationals in August. The only problem was, the nationals were in Vancouver, which meant airfare, a hotel room and eating out. I figured it was going to cost close to two thousand bucks, and where was I going to get that kind of money? Between new equipment and extra lessons, I hadn't managed to save much from my summer job. I couldn't ask Mom for it. She had enough financial problems. Plus, if she had an extra two thousand bucks, she would probably spend it to save the Tree.

The bus lurched down the dark highway. It smelled of diesel fumes and cheap perfumed soap from the tiny onboard bathroom. My legs were twice as long as the space between the rows of seats and cramped up no matter how I bent and twisted them. I drifted in and out of an uncomfortable doze. Visions of the Archibald Cross Memorial Cup played in my mind. I had visions of beating Rex, hoisting the cup and discovering a million-dollar check hidden inside it. I had visions of arriving at the nationals in style, with first-class airfare, a luxury hotel room and brand-new equipment.

I dreamed that by winning that cup, all my problems would be solved.

The Thursday evening two weeks after the provincials and one week before the Archibald Cross Memorial Tournament, I took some time off training to set up for the black-tie fundraiser. The tickets to the concert were selling like crazy, and Maddy's mom felt confident they'd have enough money to make the $100,000 payment that was due in August.

Maddy and her mom had rounded up a bunch of girls to decorate the place. They were busy arranging bouquets of flowers on the tables in the common room, stringing patio lanterns up on the verandah and planting tiki torches around the pool. Rex's dad had recruited Rex and me to set up the stage and the rented sound equipment on the lawn near the pool deck.

"A little more to the left with that speaker, boys!" Mr. Hunter shouted, his cuff links glinting. "All right, set her down!"

We lowered the speaker, heavy as a lead safe, onto a wooden platform next to the stage.

"One more to go. You boys need a break?" Mr. Hunter asked.

"Naw, I'm good," said Rex. He flashed a smile at the girls tying garlands of flowers to the deck chairs around the pool. Ever since he had won the provincials, Rex had attained the status of Greek god among the girls at the club. The only one who didn't throw herself at him was Maddy.

"How about you, Connor?" asked Mr. Hunter.

"Let's get it done," I said. I hated taking orders from Mr. Hunter, but I bit my tongue and reminded myself I wasn't doing it for him. I was doing it for Maddy, and for the club.

As night fell, we continued working under the beam of the floodlights. Finally the stage was assembled, and all the sound and light checks came up positive. The girls finished their decorating, and we stood back together to admire our work.

"This is wonderful," said Mrs. Sharma. She put one arm around Maddy and the other around me. I felt awkward because I was drenched in sweat and probably had B.O. But I put my arm around her shoulder, the way I would hug a friendly aunt at a family get-together. It seemed as if that's what she expected. Now the three of us were linked, with Maddy's arm around her mom's waist and my arm around her mom's shoulder. We stood so close that the back of my hand brushed against Maddy's upper arm. Under the moon and stars, that small touch felt intimate.

"Alanis is really excited about this," said Mr. Hunter. "She can't wait to perform."

"I can't thank you enough," said Mrs. Sharma.

"You don't need to thank me," said Mr. Hunter. "This club is a very special place, for all of us."

He had lowered his voice and put on that tone that made his words sound *deep* and *sincere*. We just stood there, not knowing what to say that wouldn't sound corny.

Then Mr. Hunter spoke in his normal businesslike voice again.

"Now, I know you don't want to talk about this, but we all remember what happened before the last fundraiser," he said.

"I'm sure that's not—" Mrs. Sharma began.

"I know," said Mr. Hunter. "It was a random act of vandalism. Still, I've asked my security guard from the office to keep an eye on things tonight. He'll do a drive-by on the street every hour. If he sees anything suspicious, he's to contact the police."

"I appreciate that," Mrs. Sharma said. "But it's really not necessary."

"It is necessary," Mr. Hunter said. "For everyone's peace of mind."

There was no arguing with Mr. Hunter. There was nothing left to set up, either, so our little group began to disperse. Mrs. Sharma and Maddy went back to the clubhouse to shut things down for the night. Some of the girls headed out to the bike racks. Other kids walked up the street toward the bus stop. I went to the locker room to get my running shoes and then sat down on the front steps of the club to change footwear for the jog home.

"Happy to give you a lift, Connor," Mr. Hunter said as he came down the steps and headed toward his Mercedes-Benz.

"I gotta train," I said. "But thanks."

"You a runner? What's your time for a five-mile run?" Mr. Hunter shot the question at me. Everything was a competition to this guy.

"About thirty-three minutes," I said.

"Not bad," said Mr. Hunter. "Rex runs it in thirty. Well, see you at the party."

I watched his Benz take off down the street. I was feeling as if I'd never be as good as Rex at anything when Maddy came up behind me.

"He's full of bull," she said. "Rex has never run five miles in his life."

"How do you know?" I turned to look up at her.

"His coach told me. He keeps trying to get Rex to take up running, and Rex won't do it. He's good, yeah. But he's lazy."

I could have jumped up and hugged her, but at that moment her mom walked out the door.

"Come on, Maddy. Let's get home." Mrs. Sharma swept her daughter toward the Jetta. "See you tomorrow, Connor."

"See you."

I sprinted to the end of the block, then fell into a strong, steady pace that I could maintain all the way home. I didn't know why it was so satisfying to know that Rex's dad was a liar and a braggart. But it was. It felt even better knowing that Maddy saw right through him.

chapter ten

I tossed and turned all night. Mom came down from the Tree and sat at the kitchen table until way past midnight, going over papers for her next day's meeting at city hall. It wasn't so much the light from the kitchen that kept me awake. It was thinking about Quinte and those scumbags in his gang, the kids who had wrecked the fundraising auction. What if they did the same thing to the concert? Sure, the security guard would be passing by every hour, but was that enough? I wished I had volunteered to sleep over at the club. That way I could have kept an eye on things personally.

I felt off kilter and anxious on my jog to the club the next morning. But when I arrived, everything looked fine. The street stirred with the regular activity of people driving to work and parents walking their kids to school. I did some stretching on the grass in front of the clubhouse and waited until Maddy and her mom pulled up. Mrs. Sharma waved and smiled a big, nervous smile as she came up the walkway. She was trying to act like nothing could possibly go wrong. But I noticed she was grasping her daughter's hand tightly as she fit the key into the lock and opened the door.

The club was quiet. Nothing looked amiss. Without saying a word, we headed up the stairs to the common room. It wasn't until I stepped into the room that my stomach unclenched. The place looked just as the girls had left it. The tables were set with white tablecloths, candles and bouquets of flowers. The patio lanterns dangled cheerily from the eaves of the verandah.

Mrs. Sharma let out a half-laugh, half-sigh and flopped into the nearest chair.

"Thank goodness," she said. She shook her head. "I don't know what I expected."

"I do," said Maddy. She squeezed her mom's shoulder.

Mrs. Sharma took a few seconds to collect herself.

"Well, good," she said finally. "Let's get this day started. We'll open up the courts, but we'll keep the pool and the common room off limits until this evening. Connor, you'd better run down to the pool and make sure everything's okay there."

"I'll come with you," said Maddy.

We didn't exactly run to the pool. We ambled along instead, basking in the morning sun. Halfway down the white-pebble path, she slipped her hand into mine. She didn't say anything, just let her fingers rest in my palm. Blood rushed to my head so fast and strong, I didn't dare look at her in case I grabbed her and started kissing her.

From this distance, our view of the pool was blocked by a row of bushes and a chain-link fence. But as we got closer, I could make out the shapes of the stage and the sound system we'd set up the night before. A cold feeling stole over me.

I dropped Maddy's hand.

"What is it?" she asked.

"Something's wrong."

I picked up my pace and started to run. As I burst through the gate, I saw the shattered stage lights, the ripped-out wires of the sound system and the speakers, sunk at the bottom of the swimming pool. The door to the pool shed was smashed open. A barrel of chlorine lay on its side on the pool deck, empty. Obviously, someone had dumped it into the pool. Thousands of dollars' worth of equipment lay drowned and ruined.

"I'm gonna kill them!" I shouted. "I'm gonna pound their heads in!"

Maddy ran up to me and grabbed my wrists.

"Stop it, Connor," she said. "We have to call the police. Oh my god, my poor mom."

Mrs. Sharma called the police. Then she called Mr. Hunter. He told her he was shocked. He explained there had been a false alarm at his office the night before, which had stopped the security guard from coming around to check on the club. He promised to try to get Alanis Morissette to come anyway. With a superhuman effort, we might be able to clean away the wreckage and set up a new stage. But Mr. Hunter called back half an hour later and said Alanis wouldn't come. She was concerned about security.

I knew I should have slept at the club that night.

The police took everything more seriously this time. Two fundraisers ruined in the space of two months had to be more than a coincidence.

"Do you know of anyone who would want to target the club?" they kept asking Maddy's mom as she paced around the office, chewing her nails. Mrs. Sharma was always so neat and well put together—not the kind of person who chewed her fingernails.

"I don't know," she said. "I don't know why. I don't know who. Oh my god, who would do this?"

Maddy and I sent out emails to people who had bought tickets, put up a cancellation notice on the website and a Closed sign on the clubhouse door. But as soon as I got a chance, I took Maddy aside where her mom and the cops couldn't hear us.

"Let's tell them," I said.

"We can't," said Maddy. "What about Quinte?"

"What about him?" I was so mad, I didn't care what happened to the dumb kid.

"Those other kids are going to lie and weasel out of it, you watch. But Quinte? He's not smart enough to fool the cops. He's going to end up in jail. It's not fair. Those other kids put him up to it—you know they did," she said. "How do you think his parents are going to feel? How am I going to face them every time I see them on our street?"

"Maybe it'll make him smarten up," I said. Then I wished I hadn't, because Maddy shot me a look of disgust. I didn't want her to hate me. That would be worse than losing the club.

"I'm gonna go bash his face in," I said.

"Don't you touch him, Connor," said Maddy.

"Not Quinte," I said. "Mike Baron."

"Don't, Connor."

"I am."

I turned away from her. If I beat up Mike Baron, maybe the cops would arrest me. Then I would tell them the whole story. I'd tell them all about Quinte and Mike, and Maddy couldn't blame me because I'd only be defending myself. I thumped out the front door and ran down the stairs. My cell phone rang, and I grabbed it from my pocket reflexively, even though I didn't feel like answering it. I checked the caller ID. It was Mom.

"Hi, Mom." I tried to keep my voice under control.

"Connor, thank goodness I got you. I need you to bring me a file from my desk."

"What? Mom, I'm busy."

"Don't sound so annoyed at me, Connor. This is important. It's a blue folder, and it's labeled *Natural Heritage Regulations*. I'm pretty sure it's on my desk. If not, it's in the filing cabinet right next to the desk."

A bunch of jerks had just destroyed the last chance of saving my club, and she was worried about natural heritage regulations?

"I can't, Mom. I'm busy. Besides, it'll take me half an hour to run home."

"Take a cab, Connor. I told you, this is important."

A cab? Mom couldn't afford a cab.

"What do you mean, *a cab*, Mom?"

"Connor, I'm at the Heritage Committee meeting at city hall. I have to give a presentation in half an hour, and I need you to do this for me."

And then I remembered why she'd been up half the night. Today the Heritage Committee was holding its first debate on whether to save the Tree.

"Okay, Mom, I'll be there." I hung up and called a cab. But I vowed that as soon as I was done, I would take my revenge on Mike.

chapter eleven

The room at city hall was packed. There were lots of people I recognized from the neighborhood, and lots of others I didn't know, many of them dressed in suits and ties.

A bunch of city politicians sat around a U-shaped table. In the middle was another table, where people sat to give their presentations. A guy was sitting there now, talking about "density guidelines" and "community design plans" and "easement agreements." I listened for a couple of minutes, but I couldn't make much sense of it.

"How's it going?" I whispered to Mom, sliding onto the bench beside her and passing her the folder.

"Hard to say," she whispered back.

All the people from my street were clustered together in one section of the audience, while all the people in business suits were sitting in a separate clump. One of them looked familiar from behind. He was tall with broad shoulders and had on a dark blue suit. A glint of gold flashed at his wrists. I leaned over to look at his face. Sure enough, it was Mr. Hunter.

"What's Rex's dad doing here?" I asked.

"Who?"

I pointed him out.

"That's Blaine Hunter," said Mom. "The chief executive officer."

"Chief executive officer of what?"

"Huntsboro. The development company. Do you know him?"

"Yeah. From the tennis club," I whispered. "You mean he's the guy who wants to cut down the Tree?"

"Not just the Tree," she answered. "They're acquiring property all over town. High-end condo developments. Big profits."

Now I had one more reason to dislike Rex's dad, as if I needed one.

"I gotta go," I said.

"Thanks for this." She patted the folder in her lap and gave me a kiss on the cheek.

"Good luck." If I couldn't beat Rex on the tennis court, maybe she could beat his dad at city hall.

I still had half a mind to hunt down Mike Baron, but instead I turned toward the Rideau Canal and started jogging back to the tennis club. I couldn't stop thinking about Rex's dad wanting to cut down the old oak tree and build his high-end condos.

Big profits. Big profits. The words repeated themselves in my head as my feet pounded the pavement. *They're acquiring property all over town. Big profits.*

Big profits. Then the words from the police came into my mind. *Do you know anyone who would want to target the club?*

Big profits. Big profits.

Do you know anyone who would want to target the club?

Mike and his gang had trashed the club twice, but why on the nights of the fundraisers? Wasn't that kind of planning a bit too smart for those idiots? And if Mike wanted to vandalize the place, why not wreck the tennis courts? That would do more harm to his opponents, like Rex and me, by throwing us off our training. Why attack the pool and the common room? It didn't make sense. And what about the fifty bucks? Did Mike pay Quinte fifty bucks? Or did someone else pay Mike, Quinte and the rest of the guys fifty bucks each to do their dirty work?

Why would someone want to sabotage the club's fundraisers? I could think of only one reason. To drive the club into bankruptcy. If the club went bankrupt, the property would go up for sale. It was prime riverfront real estate in the heart of the city.

It was the perfect spot for a high-end condo development.

Big profits. Big profits.

They're acquiring property all over town.

Do you know anyone who would want to target the club?

By the time I'd finished my run, I knew.

I burst into the clubhouse. Maddy was sitting alone in the office.

"Maddy, I know who did it," I said.

"Connor, what are you talking about?"

"Just hang on and listen."

I explained my theory. Rex's dad had paid Mike and his gang to ruin the two fundraisers so the club would go bankrupt and he could buy the property. She didn't say anything at first. Then she walked to a filing cabinet and pulled out a file folder. She opened it and laid it on the desk in front of me.

"Huntwin Equity Ltd.?" I read the logo at the top of the letterhead. "What is it?"

"It's the company we owe money to. The company that financed the club's debt," she said. She leafed through the papers and finally pointed to a signature at the bottom of one of the pages. "Blaine Hunter, CEO Huntwin Equity Ltd."

"Rex's dad?" I said.

"Yeah."

"He's the guy you owe the mortgage to?"

"His company, yeah."

"That means..."

"Exactly," said Maddy. "It means if we can't pay the loan, Rex's dad takes over the club."

"Then he comes in, bulldozes it and builds condos," I said.

"Yeah," said Maddy. "What a slimeball."

I wasn't sure what to say next. But it didn't matter. I was interrupted before I could say anything.

"That's enough of that language, Madhavi."

I turned in the direction of the voice. Maddy's mother stood in the doorway.

"Mom!" Maddy turned. Her mom walked over to the desk, closed the folder and put it back in the filing cabinet.

"That's enough of this too," she said.

"But Mom, Mr. Hunter—"

Mrs. Sharma interrupted her. "Mr. Hunter has been very generous toward this club. The reason his company holds our loan is because he offered the refinancing on better terms than any bank would give us."

"But doesn't that prove—" Maddy began.

"And, he bent over backward to help with the fundraiser," Mrs. Sharma said. "He booked Alanis Morissette for us."

"How do we know that he really booked her?" I broke in. "Did anyone talk to her? Maybe he was just making it all up."

"Now, really, Connor," Mrs. Sharma said. "I know you're angry over what's happened. And I know you have a rivalry going on with Rex. Maybe you're a little jealous of him. It doesn't mean you can go around accusing his father of criminal acts."

"But what about the security guard?" I asked. "Isn't it strange that there just happened to be a false alarm at Mr. Hunter's office last night? So the security guard couldn't come by and check on the club?"

"Connor, that's enough," said Mrs. Sharma. "I've spoken with Mr. Hunter, and he is doing his best to discuss some kind of a loan extension with his management team. We'll just have to sit tight and hope for the best. In the meantime, it doesn't do us any good to be throwing around accusations about Mr. Hunter. I do not want to hear them repeated outside of this room. Do you understand me?"

I understood her, all right. I understood that I would lose my job at the club if I went to the police with my suspicions about Mr. Hunter. I would lose my membership and my place to train. And I would probably lose my chance to ever go out with her daughter.

I nodded and looked at the floor.

"Connor, I appreciate the fact that you care about this club. I really do." Mrs. Sharma put her hand on my shoulder. "I appreciate that you were trying to help. But please, leave it to me. All right?"

"Okay," I said, still looking at the floor.

Mrs. Sharma left, closing the door behind her. Maddy came and crouched down in front of me. She looked into my face.

"We're right about this, Connor," she said. I looked into her eyes. They were brown and soft and smart and beautiful.

"I know," I said. "But what are we going to do?"

chapter twelve

Maddy decided to go and talk to Quinte. Meanwhile, I had a half-baked idea of finding Mike Baron and punching him in the face until he confessed everything. But when I tracked Mike down, he was hanging out with a bunch of tough guys at the mall. Mad as I was, I figured a five-on-one fistfight wasn't going to do anything for my case or my tennis career. In the end I called Maddy, and we met up at her place.

"We were right," she said as we sat down on the curb outside her house.

"What did Quinte say?"

"Basically, Rex's dad paid them. He was a little garbled, but that was the gist of it."

"I knew it," I said. "I bet Mr. Hunter remembered Mike from the Rideau Club."

After all, Rex and his dad had been members there for years. Probably the only reason Mr. Hunter had switched to our club a year ago was to get enough inside information to destroy it.

"I tried to get Quinte to go and talk to the police," Maddy said, "but he got all freaked out. He thought that I was going to turn *him* into the police and that he was going to go to jail. I tried to explain, but... you know how he is."

"Yeah." I picked up a pebble and threw it down the sewer grate at my feet.

"That big loan payment is due the Monday after next," Maddy said. "A hundred thousand bucks."

"What happens if you miss the payment?"

"They call in the loan."

"And that's it?"

She nodded.

"End of the club. Unless Mr. Hunter gives us an extension."

"Like that's gonna happen," I said.

I pelted another pebble down the sewer grate. I couldn't stand this. The Hunters were beating me—beating me again.

"There's got to be something we can do," I said.

Maddy gave me a bitter smile. "You got a hundred grand lying around?"

"I wish," I said. "Do you?"

She shrugged. "There's always the Archibald Cross."

The Archibald Cross Memorial Tournament was scheduled for Friday. My mom had the day off work, but she wasn't coming to watch me play. She needed to be at city hall, where the city politicians would be taking their final vote on whether or not to save the Tree.

On Thursday evening, I was lacing up my runners on the front steps of the club when I bumped into Rex. He was heading out to his motorcycle, and the usual bunch of girls was hanging around, hoping he would invite one of them for a ride.

I'd been avoiding Rex all week. I really wanted to confront him and ask him if he knew what his dad was doing to the club. But of course I couldn't do that, being under strict orders from Mrs. Sharma.

"Going out for a run?" Rex asked casually.

"Yeah," I said. "Your dad says you're pretty fast."

I couldn't resist goading him.

Rex shrugged.

"Y'know." He flashed a fake-modest smile at the girls.

"Your dad told me you run five miles in thirty minutes."

Rex shrugged again. "Yeah, that's about right."

"But then I heard from someone else that you've never run a five-mile race in your life. So..."

I let the idea hang there, that his old man was a liar. The girls fell silent, watching him.

"Is that right?" asked Rex. "You wanna go? Right now?"

"Sure. Five miles?"

"You're on."

Rex pulled a pair of running shoes out of his tennis bag. They looked brand-new. Hopefully it was a sign that Maddy was right—his coach had made him buy them, but he had never actually used them. Otherwise he really was a hotshot runner, and I was in for another "drubbing."

Rex and I took off at a good clip down the first block. I matched him stride for stride. He slowed down as soon as he rounded the corner, out of sight of the girls. It was a pace I could have kept up all day and night, but I wasn't about to let Rex set the pace. For once, we were going to compete on my terms.

The downhill slope made it an easy run from the club to the Rideau Canal. We dodged traffic across Colonel By Drive, then hit the bike path, which paralleled the canal all the way downtown. I kept up my pace, even though we weren't running downhill anymore. Rex matched my stride, and we went weaving past the jock moms pushing their sport-utility strollers and the commuter cyclists in business suits, their suit jackets flapping in the wind behind them.

We rounded the bend at the University of Ottawa campus, where a mural on one of the buildings created the optical illusion of a huge pair of watching eyes. The mural was a landmark for me, a gigantic spectator. Sometimes, if there was no one else around, I would wave to it on my morning run. I could sense Rex beginning to flag, lagging half a step behind me, then a full step. I was tempted to speed ahead, to leave Rex in my dust for once. But how did I know he wouldn't cheat, double back early and beat me to the club? I wanted to keep him in my sights. I wanted to push him. I wanted him to feel the run in every muscle tomorrow morning.

We tagged the Laurier Avenue Bridge and turned. Heading back, I could feel him

113

dragging down the pace. I played him like a fish on a hook. I slowed down a little to let him keep up. Then I sped up to make him push his limits. At last we left the bike path and wove through the side streets toward the club. Now I knew there was no shortcut he could take to cheat me out of a win. I put on the jets to pull ahead of him. Rex must have had some energy reserves left, though, because he pumped his arms and matched my stride. We rounded the last corner before the club. The girls were still hanging out on the front steps, drinking soda. I broke into a sprint. My thighs screamed, my legs burned, but I loved the pain because it meant I was winning. I heard Rex's heavy breathing behind me, but I crossed the club's walkway a full three strides ahead of him.

The way I felt, you'd think I had won the Boston Marathon.

"Good run, Connor." Rex thumped me on the back. I was bent over double, trying to stop wheezing.

"Good run," I said. And I meant it.

"Hey, a bunch of us are going out tonight," Rex said when he'd recovered his breath. "Want to come?"

"No thanks. Tournament tomorrow."

"Oooh, yeah. *Biiig* tournament." Rex laughed.

I looked at him, so suave and self-confident. Maybe he didn't believe the rumors about the hidden wealth in the Archibald Cross cup. Or maybe he was so rich he didn't care. In either case, he waved as he took off on his bike with one of the girls hanging on behind him.

Maybe the tournament didn't matter to Rex. Since it was open only to club members, it didn't affect his national ranking. Still, it mattered a lot to me. And I knew one thing—a five-mile run and an evening of partying tonight was going to make Rex a whole lot easier to beat tomorrow.

chapter thirteen

The Archibald Cross Memorial Cup gleamed in the sunlight as players milled around on the lawn of the tennis club, waiting for the tournament to begin. Beside the table that held the cup sat an old man in a navy-blue suit. He had a bald head and a thick lower lip that stuck out like the spout of a teapot. He was the executor of old Mr. Cross's will, and it was his job to award the cup to the winner of the tournament.

I said hi to Maddy as I tossed my bag on the lawn and began to stretch. But she was so focused on the match ahead that she didn't answer. She didn't even glance at Rex when he sauntered onto the lawn, wearing Ray-Bans, a blue-and-orange Nike top and coordinated shorts.

Maddy was the only girl in the tournament. Some others had tried out, but they had fallen in the elimination rounds earlier in the week. Usually, a tournament would be split into different categories for guys and girls. But in this case, since there was only one Archibald Cross Memorial Cup, everyone was competing against each other.

Heading into the quarterfinals that morning, Maddy's opponent was a lumbering, ham-fisted kid with twice her brawn and less than half her technique. If I were placing a bet, I'd have bet on Maddy. But part of me desperately and disloyally wanted her to lose the quarterfinals, because if she made the semis, I'd be slotted to play against her.

At 10:00 AM I headed onto the court for my quarterfinal match against William Sweet, a kid with a decent serve, a passable forehand and not much else going for him. For the past two weeks, I'd been working with the club pro, Armand, to add spin to my serve. I had transformed it from a powerful opening salvo into a truly deadly weapon. It did the job against William. He left the court after two sets with a stunned look on his face. I had barely broken a sweat.

Maddy made moose meat of her opponent, too, so at noon we found ourselves shaking hands across the net for the semifinal match. I wished her good luck, even though my only goal now was to knock her out and advance to the final.

I won the toss and took first serve. How to play it, I asked myself, as I dragged my heels to the baseline. My rule for playing against Maddy had always been not to cream her on the serve. But that was in practice. This was for real. And now my serve was more powerful than ever. It was a speeding, spinning missile designed to destroy my opponent on contact. I needed that weapon in my arsenal.

The best thing to do was pretend I wasn't playing against Maddy. I was playing a nameless, faceless opponent who needed to be eliminated in my ruthless drive to victory.

First serve. The ball went sizzling off my racket, hit the ground with a vicious sidespin and notched the first point of the game. I hit two more serves with the same deadly force, and I was up 40-love before Maddy even got a racket on the ball. On the final serve, Maddy managed a return, but I won the game on a backhand down the line. On a hot streak, I took the second game and muscled my way to victory in the third. By the fourth game, I really had forgotten I was playing against Maddy. She was only a moving target, and my goal was to put the ball as far away from that target as possible. My world consisted only of my body, my racket and the ball, working together in perfect harmony. Forehands, backhands, overhands, serves. The ball went singing off my racket. The points racked up until a final, beautiful backhand finished the set and I stood there dripping with sweat and surging with energy. I had won the set, 6-1.

I flopped into my chair at the sideline and squirted cold water down my throat and on my face. I toweled off the water and sweat. As I finished wiping my eyes, I glanced at the chair on the opposite side of the net. Maddy was sitting there, her jaw clenched.

"Well, that was humiliating," she muttered.

The intensity in her voice hit me like a punch in the face. Suddenly, she was real again.

"Maddy, I—"

"Forget about it," she said. "Game on, Connor."

She turned away, took a slug of water, wiped the sweat off her face and stood up to signal she was ready to play. I watched as she walked toward the baseline. I watched the way her white tennis skirt swung with her hips and brushed against the dark skin of her thighs. I saw the anger in her hunched shoulders and it seeped into me, sucking away the joy of my first-set win. I wanted to patch it up with her. I wanted to feel her fling her arms around my neck the way she had done after my win against Mike Baron.

Would it kill me to let her win a game or two?

I hadn't figured out the answer to that question when Maddy's serve rocketed past me and she went up 15-love in the first game of the second set.

Focus, Connor.

Another serve came darting at me. I lobbed it back crosscourt at three-quarter speed. I was playing for time. I hadn't made up my mind yet what to do. My body ached to get back into that place of perfect harmony with the ball and my racket. I knew I could slip into it again if I just let myself. But I wasn't sure I wanted to, not against Maddy.

Maddy pummeled the ball down the line. I reached it with a lunge that sent it airborne like a baseball pop fly. Maddy smashed an overhead. I spun around, but it was too late to do anything. The ball caromed away. A cheer erupted from the lawn behind me.

I turned. Every girl in the club must have been there to watch Maddy fight for a spot in the finals.

She served again. I sent a return low and fast down the line. She netted the ball. 30-15. It didn't shake her. She was in good form on the next serve. Confidently, she arced her body back and whipped it forward, sending all her power into the ball.

Ace.

I couldn't get a racket on it.

40-15. Game point.

Maddy's serve came sailing into the forecourt. I sent it back with a shot to the baseline. Maddy whipped it crosscourt to my backhand. I hammered it to her backhand. She nailed it down the line, but I got there in time and smoked it crosscourt. Maddy reached it and kept the rally alive. The crowd began to shout and whistle as we exchanged blows, drawing out the rally to ten shots, twelve shots, fourteen, sixteen.

I thought I had her trapped on a deep backhand and came to the net to finish her off. But Maddy sent the ball looping over my head. I ran like a madman but couldn't reach it. It bounced just inside the baseline and went flying over the fence.

Game, Maddy.

A cheer went up from the crowd. Somehow, I felt like cheering too. Maddy looked so happy. She held her shoulders straight and bounced lightly on the balls of her feet.

I'm happy for her. How screwed up is that? I asked myself as I walked to the baseline and prepared to serve.

Really screwed up. You just lost, numbskull.

Yeah, but Maddy won.

Really, really screwed up.

Okay, here's the deal, I told myself. I'll go back to my old rule for playing Maddy. Make it a fair game but don't cream her on the serve. Don't humiliate her. I can still win.

I tossed the ball and drew my racket back to strike. But I had spent the past two weeks honing my supersonic serve, and changing it now wasn't as easy as pressing a reset button. I missed my timing and sent the ball into the net. I botched the second serve as well. Suddenly I was down love-15 on a double fault. Talk about humiliation.

My next serve was a creampuff, and Maddy shredded it with a hit down the line. My concentration busted, I double-faulted on the next point, making it love-40. Triple break point. The crowd full of girls was chanting Maddy's name. I couldn't think straight. Somehow I sent a serve over the net and went through the mechanical motions of a rally. But I lost the final point on a badly placed shot that bounced wildly out of bounds, and Maddy went up 2-0 in the second set.

Before I knew it, the next game was over, and Maddy was up 3-0. The girls in the crowd were shouting hysterically. I grabbed a drink of water and stared at them until I caught sight of Armand standing off to one side.

He saw me looking at him and raised his hands in an exaggerated shrug as if asking, *What the hell?*

I shrugged back.

He made a motion with his right arm that said, *Use your serve, man.*

I turned away and walked toward the baseline. Use my serve? Of course, use my serve. At 0-3, now was the time, if ever, to make a comeback.

The question was, did I want to?

Maybe I should let Maddy win. She needed the money—if there was any—to save the club. I only needed it for my own career. Didn't she deserve it more?

I bounced the ball hard against the clay court surface and felt it spring back into the cup of my palm. I knew I could make it dance and howl out there on the court, if I wanted to. All I needed was to want it.

Serve it up, Connor. What's it going to be?

Maybe I should let her win. But what would happen after that? It was only the semifinal match. No one was walking away with the cup until they'd won the final. And the final would probably be against Rex. Rex wouldn't throw the game for Maddy. If I let the weaker player advance just because I liked her or felt sorry for her, there was all the more chance that Rex would hoist the trophy at the end of the day. Once again it would be Rex the winner, Connor the loser.

Maddy must have known her chances of beating Rex were slim if she did advance to the final. But she was out there giving it her best shot, because it was the only thing she could do. Maybe I didn't have a better chance of beating Rex than Maddy did, but I had to try. I had to give it my best shot too.

I threw a perfect toss and struck the ball square and hard. It went sizzling past Maddy. She didn't even have a chance to stick out her racket for a block shot. I served another smoker and then another, ended on an ace and won the game. I stole the next game from her while she was still reeling and deployed my serve in the following game to tie up the set, 3-3.

The girls in the crowd fell silent. Maddy hunched her shoulders as she walked to the baseline. But I couldn't let her anger or my guilt throw me off. If Maddy were a weaker player, I could have toyed around with her. I could have eased off, let her score a few points, and then come from behind again to win. But she was too good for that. If I wanted to beat her, I needed to fight for every point.

I broke Maddy's serve in the next game and held serve in the following game to bring the score to 5-3 in my favor. Maddy fought for a comeback and narrowed the gap to 5-4. But then it was my turn to serve again. Win this game, and the semifinal victory was mine.

I sent a serve scorching across the net. Maddy blocked it, but it popped up high and soft. I sliced it back with a volley into the left forecourt at a devious angle. Her feet couldn't take her there fast enough to get a racket on it. 15-love. The next serve burned past her. 30-love. She fought back on the following point, blocked my serve and forced me into a long, hard baseline rally. I sent a forehand over with too much power and not enough topspin, and it landed just long of the baseline. 30-15. I aced the next serve and went up to 40-15. Match point.

I stood at the baseline and drew in my breath for one last serve. I forced myself not to think about Maddy, or the cup, or the fabled cash prize, or Rex Hunter, or anything beyond the ball in my hand and the circuit that connected my brain to my racket. *Play one point. One point.*

I served hard into the deuce court. The block came back down the line. I whipped it crosscourt and set myself up for the return. I picked up the ball at the baseline and reamed it crosscourt again. She reached it with the tip of her racket. I charged the net as it came floating over. I hammered it into the far corner, saw it hit the ground at the junction of the baseline and the side-line, saw Maddy lunge for it and miss, saw the ball skim out of reach.

I jumped in the air with my racket over my head and let out a whoop. A whoop for clinching the match with a beautiful shot. A whoop for advancing to the finals, for coming one step closer to the silver cup.

But Maddy was hunched over on her side of the court, her hands on her knees, her head hanging down.

I wanted to go over to her but couldn't. It was bad form to cross into an opponent's court. Instead I waited at the net for the final handshake, knowing she had too much class to brush it off.

At last she came to the net and held out her hand. She was crying.

"Maddy, I..."

"It's okay, Connor. Good game."

"I wasn't trying to humiliate you," I said.

"It's not that." She bit her lip and looked away. "It's the club."

She pulled her hand out of mine and walked off the court. Reaching the lawn, she broke into a run. I saw a couple of her friends step out of the crowd and follow her into the clubhouse. I went after her, but by the time I reached the clubhouse, she was hiding out in the girls' locker room.

I stood alone in the front hall of the tennis club and wondered how being a winner could make you feel like so much of a loser.

chapter fourteen

The final match between Rex and me got underway at six o'clock that evening. Rex had faced an unexpectedly tough opponent in the semis. He was a kid named Sergei who'd recently come from Russia with his parents. Sergei had won the first set against Rex and pushed the second to a tiebreaker. I'd caught some of the third set and seen enough of Sergei's massive forehand and killer backhand to be thankful I hadn't faced him.

Before the finals began, Armand yanked me aside.

"Make Rex run, Connor," he whispered. "He's got no legs left."

The crowd on the lawn had swelled since my semifinal against Maddy, blocking my view of the executor and his gleaming silver cup. Most of the competitive juniors and their parents were there. There were also gray-haired old-timers who remembered Mr. Cross and were curious to see who would win his cup.

Rex won the toss and took first serve. I crouched in ready position at the baseline, awaiting the onslaught of his serve-and-volley attack.

But the serve and volley never came. Rex stayed at the baseline while I whipped the return crosscourt. He whipped it back and dug in at the baseline, pummeling me with forehands and backhands, trying to kill me with power shots. This was my kind of game, a baseline rally. I could go on like this all day. But why was Rex playing my kind of game?

Rex was a serve-and-volley guy. He was a guy with tricks and technique, a guy who was at his best flitting up and down the court, dancing circles around his opponent. What was he doing playing baseline tennis? There was only one answer. Flitting around the court took speed and energy. It took legs. After the five-mile run yesterday, the night of partying and the marathon match against Sergei, Rex had no legs left. Armand was right.

I knew what I had to do. Grind him down. Wear him out. I sent him running from corner to corner on the rallies, and though I lost the first three games, by the fourth Rex was flagging. I took three games in a row, pushed the score in the first set to 5-6, then 6-6, then lost a squeaker in the tiebreaker. I had never come so close to beating Rex in my life.

As I passed him switching sides, Rex winced with every step. If only I could win the next set, I might be able to outlast him in the third and win the match through sheer endurance.

By the second game of the second set, Rex's pace was half a step slower than at the beginning of the match. By the third game, he was a full step off his speed. He missed balls he should have reached. He gave up on shots he should have returned.

Strategy, now, was worth as much as strength. In the first set, I'd hit a number of balls out of bounds because I was trying to make him run to reach them. Now, since he could cover less court, I had more room to play with. I didn't need to aim so close to the sidelines. That meant I would lose fewer points on unforced errors. And as I cut down on my rate of unforced errors, Rex began racking them up. He was getting frustrated. He started double-faulting on serves and sending shots into the net.

I broke his serve in the second set to bring the score to 5-4 in my favor. All I needed to win the set was to hold serve on the final game.

I served into the glare of the evening sun, but even that didn't bother me. My serve was flowing on a circuit of pure muscle memory. I felt as though I could have hit it blindfolded, like the pinball wizard in that old song by The Who. At set point, I fired a beautiful backhand down the line, and Rex didn't even run for it. He just turned and walked away, shaking his head, wondering how he could have lost a set against the same kid he had "drubbed" a month before at the Donalda Club.

We were tied at one set each. I sensed I was close to victory. I could feel the Archibald Cross Memorial Cup pulling me like a magnet toward the finish line.

But Rex wasn't about to give up. He might not have cared about the cup. He might not have known or cared about the hidden money. But he cared about his pride. And pride meant a lot to Rex. Maybe he was even mad at me for suckering him into running five miles the night before. When he stepped to the baseline for the first serve of the final set, he sledgehammered the ball into my court so fast I could almost hear it laughing at me as it sped for the sideline and skimmed out of reach.

Game on, Rex, I thought. *Here's to the last man standing.*

I couldn't break Rex on the first game, but I made him work for every point. We reached deuce three times before he put me away with a lucky shot that tipped the net and dribbled over. The next game, I used my serve as a weapon of retaliation. I drew him into long rallies that made him run corner to corner. I lured him into the forecourt at 40-15 and put him away with a sweet passing shot that waved bye-bye as it sailed past him.

By the time the score hit 3-3, Rex was getting sick of being pushed around.

He double-faulted on the opening point, smashing it twice into the net. On the next point, he smashed his first serve into the net and sliced the second serve wide of the court. It was love-30, and I hadn't yet lifted a racket. He flung a tennis ball at the chain-link fence. It seemed to help him calm down, because by the time he retrieved the ball, he'd gotten himself under control. His next serve struck the court inbounds, but it had no sizzle. I reamed it back down the line, where his tired legs couldn't take him. 0-40. Triple break point.

Rex fired a serve to my backhand. I blocked it back, playing it safe. He slammed it crosscourt, but I was waiting for it. I rammed it down the line, making him run to reach it. He fired it back down the line.

Crosscourt was the obvious shot for me now. All match long, I had been sending Rex corner to corner. As the ball came toward me, I watched Rex anticipate my play and commit himself to the crosscourt shot. Then I fired it down the line instead. He pivoted halfway around, but he never had a chance.

Game, Connor.

I was up a break, leading 4-3 in the third and final set.

I held serve on the next game, held on to it with my fingernails, while Rex threw everything he had at me. We beat each other up in baseline rallies. He took me to deuce twice before his ball bit the net and his game bit the dust. Bending over to catch my breath, I silently thanked Sergei and the girls who had taken Rex out partying the night before for wearing him down enough to give me a fighting chance.

I was up 5-3 now, with Rex serving. I needed to break him again to win the cup. He needed to hold me off to stay alive.

His first serve flashed into my service court. I played it safe with a return down the middle, an opening salvo in a baseline rally. But when I looked up from my stroke, I realized that Rex was no longer at the baseline. His red, sweaty face grinned at me from just beyond the net. Too late for me to react, he hit a drop shot and the ball stopped dead in my forecourt.

15-0.

Rex was staking his last stand on the serve and volley.

I stood at the baseline, waiting for his next serve, frantically trying to figure out what to do. He would kill a block shot or anything lightweight heading to center court. My only options were to drill it down the line or pop it up over his head.

The ball came walloping to my backhand, and I opted to drill it down the line. But I drilled it into the net instead. 30-0.

I had to get a grip. I couldn't let the cup slip away, slip into Rex's hands. I couldn't let him psych me out with his rush to the net. No, I told myself. The cup is mine. I can feel it pulling me to the finish. I'm only a few points away.

Rex's next serve came hard and fast. He rushed the net again, but I slipped it past him down the line. 30-15.

I could practically hear him grinding his teeth as he lined up again to serve. He smashed the first one into the net, then rifled off a cautious second serve. This time he stayed at the baseline while I hammered it to his backhand. He whipped it back to mine. Soon we were into a baseline rally. All at once I could feel the long day of tennis dragging me down. I could feel the ache in my shoulders and the burn in my legs. I knew I had to win this game or my chances would dwindle with every additional point I played.

I pummeled him for all I was worth, but Rex wasn't giving up. He hit one deep to the corner that I thought I couldn't reach. I lunged for it anyway, and somehow I got a racket on it. It went looping up high, a crazy moonball, and touched down in the back of beyond, just inside Rex's baseline. The ball took a weird sideways bounce that threw off Rex's timing. He stabbed at it, but his shot barely had enough power to clear the net. I rushed forward and chopped the ball into the forecourt. Rex ran for it, dove, reached it in time to send it up in a soft arc over the net, so soft that it floated to my racket. I hammered it into an empty space in the back corner of his court, so far away that Rex couldn't dream of reaching it. 30-30.

Rex picked himself up and brushed the dirt from the clay court off his shorts. He walked gingerly back to the baseline, as though it hurt to move. I bounced on the spot, kicked up my heels, tried to convince my body to stay limber. I was two points away from the cup.

Rex's serve came in with a vicious spin. It was all I could do to stick a racket out and block it to get the ball into play. Rex was moving forward for the serve and volley. But his slow legs trapped him in no-man's-land, too far from the net for an effective shot. He slapped the ball with an awkward stroke, trying to keep it alive. I scooped it up and aimed it down the line, deep into the corner. Rex turned but couldn't get back in time.

30-40.

Match point.

I walked to the baseline. Flexed my legs in a deep squat. Wiped the sweat from my forehead with the back of my arm. Closed my eyes. Breathed. Opened my eyes again.

I couldn't let myself think about what it meant to win this game. It didn't only mean taking home the cup. It didn't only mean pocketing the prize money, if there was any. It meant payback against Rex for all the times he had whupped me. It meant taking down the guy whose dad was plotting to destroy my club.

It meant showing the Hunters a kid like me could beat them. That would be sweeter than any silver cup.

The serve came barreling toward me. I parried with a backhand that sent the ball toward center court. I knew an instant later it was the wrong move. With a last burst of adrenaline, Rex leapt toward the net for the serve and volley. Racket outstretched, he zeroed in on the ball's flight path. But the ball, at the last moment, nicked the top of the net. And instead of hitting Rex's racket, it hopped over it and touched ground on the court behind him.

Rex turned. He flailed. The ball was still alive, still on its first bounce. Rex took a whack at it, and it sailed high into the dusk, over the fence that encircled the tennis court. It landed somewhere in the grass, but no one cared where because it was all over now. Rex let his racket fall to the ground. As for me, I fell to my knees on that rough clay court and raised my arms over my head with a cry of victory.

chapter fifteen

I worked my way through the mass of people on the lawn, through a gauntlet of high fives and slaps on the back, until I stood in front of the table with the gleaming Archibald Cross Memorial Cup. I searched the crowd for a glimpse of Maddy, but I didn't see her anywhere. Was she still in the change room? Had she gone home? Had she seen me win against Rex? Could she even be happy for my victory?

The executor was standing at a microphone. He waited for the noise of the crowd to die down before beginning his speech.

"Ladies and gentlemen! It is my honor and privilege to award the Archibald Cross Memorial Cup to the winner of this tournament, Mr. Connor Trent."

The crowd applauded as I stepped forward and accepted the cup from the executor's hands. I hoisted it above my head. It felt heavy. Was it heavy enough to contain a bar of solid gold? I slid my fingers around the base, checking for a hidden compartment, but I couldn't feel anything. I lowered the cup and tried not to look like an ungrateful money-grubber as the executor continued his speech.

"The cup is a bequest of the late Archibald Cross, a long-time member of this club and, I know, a personal friend to many of you here today." The executor paused. The crowd gave a polite round of applause in memory of Mr. Cross. "As per the directions in the late Mr. Cross's will, the winner of the cup is also to be awarded this sealed envelope."

The crowd fell silent. I felt my stomach prickle. The executor pulled an envelope from an inside pocket of his suit jacket and handed it to me. It was made of heavy, cream-colored paper. On the front was written *To the Winner of the Archibald Cross Memorial Junior Tennis Tournament.* On the back, an old-fashioned red-wax seal held the envelope flap closed.

Suddenly, everyone in the crowd began to talk at once. I heard the words "money" and "prize" and "how much"? I was wondering the same thing myself. But before I could rip open the envelope, the executor put a steady hand on mine and leaned toward me.

"Tuck that away somewhere until you get home, son," he whispered. "In my considerable experience, sealed envelopes are best opened in private."

Mom was sitting at the kitchen table when I got home. All the files and documents about the Tree were piled in front of her, but she wasn't reading them. She was drinking a cup of black coffee, an open bottle of Bailey's Irish Cream on the table beside her, and staring into space.

It looked like it hadn't been a good day.

"We lost at city hall," she said.

"I'm sorry, Mom."

"They're starting cutting tomorrow." She wiped away a tear. I guessed from the redness around her eyes that it wasn't the first. "I can't talk about it, Connor. It makes me sick to my stomach."

I pulled up a chair and sat down opposite her. I set the Archibald Cross Memorial Cup on the table. The thing was too big to ignore.

"What's this?" she said.

"I won the tournament at the club today."

"Oh yes, your tournament. I'm sorry, honey, I forgot. Congratulations." She smiled at me. "It's a very...um...handsome cup."

"There's something else that went with it, Mom," I said. I pulled the envelope out of my tennis bag. My fingers fumbled with the seal. I didn't want to rip the envelope. It didn't seem dignified. I finally had to get a knife from the cutlery drawer, lay the envelope flat on the table and run the knife under the seal. Mom looked on, curious.

I slid out a crisp piece of paper. I could tell by its size and feel that it was a check. Written on the back was *To be used for the Purposes of the Sport of Tennis*.

I turned it over.

One hundred thousand dollars.

I stared at it, my fingers tingling. My heart thumped faster than it had in my final game against Rex.

"A hundred thousand dollars," Mom said.

"*For the Purposes of the Sport of Tennis*," I said.

She shook her head. Mom couldn't imagine how anyone could spend $100,000 on a sport. That was more than a sports car. That was more than two years of her salary.

"What are you going to do with it, Connor?"

I put the check down on the table.

"I don't know, Mom."

I thought about all the things I could buy with $100,000—lessons from the best pros, top-of-the-line gear, airfare to tournaments, training at winter camps in Florida. I thought about what Armand had said, that a year of touring on the international junior circuit would cost $100,000.

I thought about Maddy running into the clubhouse, crying.

"See, Mom," I said, "it's really complicated."

I told her then about the vandalism at the club, and how Maddy and I had figured out that Mr. Hunter was behind it. I told her about Quinte, and how we couldn't go to the police because Maddy didn't want him to go to jail. I told her how Mr. Hunter was going to take over the club if the $100,000 debt payment wasn't made by Monday.

I told her about Maddy trying to win the tournament so she could make the debt payment and save the club.

I told her about how I dreamed of playing on the international juniors circuit, and how hard it was to compete against the rich kids like Rex.

"The club pro says that touring internationally costs about a hundred grand a year. So this check"—I traced the printed numbers with my finger—"would get me one year of touring."

"Then what?" Mom asked.

"Then I'd have to figure out if I was good enough to turn pro, if I could win enough prize money to keep it going. Or if I wasn't good enough, I'd have to drop out."

"But if you're not good enough at the end of the year and you drop out, then you've thrown all that money away," Mom said.

"I know," I said. "Or I could use it—"

She finished my thought. "To save the club."

We sat there in silence, each thinking our way through it.

"You know I don't understand professional sports, Connor," Mom said finally. "But is there any other way you can still play tennis without this money?"

I'd been thinking about that too.

"I need two thousand dollars to go to the nationals this summer," I said.

"Let's say we could scrape that together."

"Okay, then if I did well at the nationals, I might get a scholarship to an American college. Play the college circuit while I got a degree. And if I did well on the circuit, then maybe I could go from there to turning pro."

"That sounds like a reasonable option," said Mom. "And you'd get an education."

I nodded. It wasn't exactly my dream come true. It wasn't jet-setting off to European tournaments and buying the latest top-end gear. And there was a chance that I would flop at the nationals and never win a scholarship. But apart from that, Mom was right. It was a reasonable option.

I wasn't sure I wanted to settle for the reasonable option. The idea of spending a hundred grand of free money on the international juniors circuit was way more appealing. But one thought held me back. Sure, I had won the tournament against Rex. But what would that victory be worth if I let his dad take over the club, bulldoze it and build condos? Who was the winner then? Blaine Hunter. The same guy who was going to cut down Mom's Tree. The same guy who'd sabotaged our fundraisers. The same guy who'd paid a bunch of teenagers to do his dirty work. The same guy who would never face justice because we couldn't prove anything against him without ratting out a frightened, mentally challenged kid.

Now, against all odds, I had a chance to stop Blaine Hunter. The hundred grand wouldn't solve all the club's debt problems, but it would at least give us enough breathing room to figure out what to do next. Was I going to let that chance slip away?

"Connor," said Mom, "it's your money. You have to decide how to spend it. But I want to tell you something. I've lived in this town a long time. And I've seen a lot of changes. And I can tell you one thing. Look around at any park you walk through, any historical building you pass on the street. Chances are, some developer, at some point in time, has wanted to rip it up or tear it down and put up a mall or a high-rise or anything else he thinks will make him an almighty buck. And the only reason those parks and historical buildings and places like your tennis club are still there is because somebody fought for them. If something is important to you, you have to fight for it. You might not always win. But you have to fight for it."

Mom was crying. I hugged her.

After she wiped away her tears, I picked up the check and tucked it in my back pocket.

I had a lot of thinking to do before the Monday deadline.

chapter sixteen

The special meeting for the club's board of directors was scheduled for ten o'clock Monday morning. I arrived to find a big boardroom-style table set up in the common room. Mrs. Sharma sat at the head of the table, with Mr. Hunter beside her. The directors sat around the table, and the ordinary club members were crowded into rows of chairs to one side.

Some heads turned when I walked into the room. Taking a cue from the executor,

I had dressed in a suit and tie. Maddy looked at me but didn't smile. I took a seat at the table. No one said anything to stop me.

Mrs. Sharma opened the meeting. She laid out the club's financial troubles. She explained the vandalism. She said the police were still investigating but hadn't made any arrests. Then she turned the floor over to Mr. Hunter.

Mr. Hunter recapped the situation with the club's debt. He said he'd held discussions with his management team about extending the repayment date.

"Regrettably, in these troubled economic times, the decision was made that deferring the loan repayment is not a viable option," he said. "This club means as much to me as it does to all of you. I'm very sorry. There's nothing I can do."

The room was silent.

Mrs. Sharma cleared her throat and said, "Unfortunately, this leaves the club little choice but to declare bankruptcy. I'd like to put forward a motion to the board—"

"Excuse me!" I jumped out of my seat. My chair fell over with a clatter.

"Yes, Connor?" asked Mrs. Sharma. Everyone stared at me.

"I just wanted to know...I mean, exactly how much is the payment? I mean, the one that's due today?" My voice cracked. My heart hammered in my throat.

Mr. Hunter smiled his fake smile. It was amazing how the guy could smile so much on the outside and be so rotten on the inside.

"Certainly, Connor," he said. He glanced down at a paper on the table in front of him. "The exact amount is ninety-nine thousand three hundred and fifty-six dollars and ninety-two cents."

He smiled again. "Though we could waive the ninety-two cents."

I reached inside my jacket pocket and pulled out the check. It seemed bigger than I remembered it, and somehow heavier. The number leapt out at me—$100,000.00. My hand trembled as I slid it across the table to Mr. Hunter.

"I think this should cover it," I said.

Mr. Hunter's smile froze for a second, then slowly collapsed. The fake-friendly twinkle dimmed from his eyes. He rose from his chair, took the check, sat down again and examined it.

Finally, he looked up.

"This appears to be in order," he said.

Mrs. Sharma squealed. Someone shouted, "What? What's this about?" The directors swarmed around Mr. Hunter. Everybody started talking at once.

But then all the noise faded into the background. Suddenly, Maddy was in my arms, her warm body pressed against me, her face burrowed into my shoulder. I kissed her long, dark hair. I held her against me. And for once, I felt like the biggest winner in the world.

epilogue

It's funny how a summer that started so badly could end so well.

The club paid for my trip to the nationals. Mrs. Sharma insisted on it after I gave my $100,000 check to Mr. Hunter. I didn't win the championship, but neither did Rex. That honor went to a hotshot from Calgary. One thing I realized at the tournament was how much my game needed to improve if I seriously hoped to compete internationally. So, as it turned out, going after a college scholarship wasn't such a bad decision after all.

I got lucky. A scout from Florida State University offered me a scholarship for the following September, provided I kept my marks up in my last year of high school. Maddy won her division at the nationals, and she got offered a scholarship to the University of Michigan. In the meantime, we'd be spending our senior year together at a special sports high school, where kids took regular classes in the morning and athletic training in the afternoon. It sounded as close to nirvana as high school could be.

When we got home from the nationals, there was more good news. The police had made a breakthrough in the vandalism case. The clue was a gold chain, which the cops had found in the grass after the outdoor stage was wrecked. The personalized engraving on the chain allowed them to trace it back to Mike Baron. When the cops confronted Mike, he didn't betray the other guys in his gang, not even Quinte.

So it turned out there was some good in Mike after all. But he *did* rat out Mr. Hunter.

Of course, Rex's dad denied everything. But when Mrs. Sharma threatened to sue him, he agreed to settle out of court for $400,000. That was the amount the club still owed to his company. With the settlement, the debt was erased and the club no longer had to worry about bankruptcy. No developer would be coming to bulldoze our tennis courts.

The last week in August, the insurance check for the vandalism of the tennis auction finally came through. I was sitting with Maddy on the bench at the back of the club, overlooking the Rideau River, when Mrs. Sharma came up and placed the check in my hand.

"It's yours, Connor," she said. "You deserve it. You deserve more than that."

I looked at the check. It was for $20,000. I felt embarrassed, but she insisted I take it. I tucked it away safely in my tennis bag. The truth was, with Maddy beside me under the late-summer sun and the sounds of rackets hitting balls in the courts all around us, I felt as though I already had more than I deserved.

I didn't know where my tennis career would take me. First to Florida. After that, maybe all over the world. But I knew that whatever happened, I could always come back here, to this club by the river, and I would feel welcome.

I couldn't help thinking that if old Mr. Cross was looking down from the afterworld, he would be proud of what I had accomplished with his prize money. Not for myself, but for the Purposes of the Sport of Tennis.

Acknowledgments

I would like to thank Gabriela Dabrowski and her mother, Wanda, for taking the time to talk to me about Gabriela's experiences on the competitive tennis circuit. As of December 31, 2012, Gabriela was ranked 309 in the world for women's singles and 134 in the world for women's doubles. She and her mother helped me understand how young athletes work their way up the ranks as they aspire to become professional tennis players. Peter Sutcliffe, the club pro at the Ottawa Tennis and Lawn Bowling Club, very graciously fielded all my questions about the sport and gave me insight into the financial challenges involved in playing at a national and international level. Peter and his son Michael (winner of the National Capital Tennis Association 2012 City Open Championships in Men's Singles and Doubles) read my manuscript and caught my technical errors before the book went to press. I owe them thanks for making me look more knowledgeable than I am. Finally, this book would never have been written without the support and inspiration of my husband, Mark, whose brainstorming over plot and character helped to shape the story. I promise to take him out for drinks with the first royalty check.

Kate Jaimet is an Ottawa author and jour-
nalist who recently began a freelance
career after many years as a daily news-
paper reporter for the *Ottawa Citizen*. Her
first book in the Orca Sports series, *Slam
Dunk*, was chosen as a Junior Library Guild
Selection and was included in the Canadian
Children's Book Centre's Best Books for
Kids & Teens. For more information, visit
www.katejaimet.com.

ALSO AVAILABLE BY
KATE JAIMET

EDGE OF FLIGHT IS THE TOUGHEST rock-climbing route Vanisha has ever faced. She has one last chance to conquer it before she moves to Vermont to start university. On her final weekend of climbing, she and her buddies Rusty and Jeb stumble on an illegal marijuana plantation. When Jeb is shot by the bikers who guard it, Vanisha must climb Edge of Flight to seek help. Will she have the courage she needs to help save Jeb?

orca sports
Slam Dunk
Kate Jaimet

9781554691326 PB

ASSISTANT COACH OF THE GIRLS' BASKETBALL
team. Sounds like an easy gig for sixteen-year-old
Salvador "Slam" Amaro. Show up, run a few drills and
pad his resumé so he can win a spot on the Ontario
Under 17 men's team. But Slam hasn't bargained on
the girls' head coach and the star point guard going
missing. With the girls facing playoff elimination, Slam
has to solve the mystery of their disappearance and
take over as head coach of the team while battling
some tough competitors for his own place on the
Ontario squad.

Titles in the Series

orca sports

orca sports

For more information on all the books
in the Orca Sports series, please visit
www.orcabook.com.